Eyewitness
VOLCANO

Vesuv. Ash rain of the eruption
(March 1944: days 22. 23. 24. 25. 26)

Skull from Herculaneum

Lava bomb

Sulphur

Gray-Milne seismograph, 1885

Carbonised bread from Pompeii

Cut peridot

Gem-quality olivine

Cut and uncut diamond

Carbonised walnuts from Pompeii

Preserved eggs from Pompeii

Body cast from Pompeii

Pele's hair

Voyager 1
space probe

Eyewitness
VOLCANO

Written by
SUSANNA VAN ROSE

Bottle melted in
eruption of
Mount Peléc

Perfume bottle
melted in eruption
of Mount Pelée

Zhang Heng's
earthquake detector

DK

Seneca, Roman philosopher who
wrote about earthquake of 62 CE

Title page from
Campi Phlegraei

Fork and pocket
watch damaged
in eruption of
Mount Pelée

DK

LONDON, NEW YORK,
MELBOURNE, MUNICH, and DELHI

Project editor Scott Steedman
Art editor Christian Sévigny
Designer Yaël Freudmann
Managing editor Helen Parker
Managing art editor Julia Harris
Production Louise Barratt
Picture research Kathy Lockley
Special photography James Stevenson
Editorial consultants Professor John Guest and Dr Robin Adams

THIS EDITION
Consultant Douglas Palmer
Editors Francesca Baines, Sue Nicholson,
Victoria Heywood-Dunne, Marianne Petrou
Art editors Catherine Goldsmith, David Ball
Managing editors Andrew Macintyre, Camilla Hallinan
Managing art editors Jane Thomas, Martin Wilson
Publishing manager Sunita Gahir
Production editors Siu Yin Ho, Andy Hilliard
Production controllers Jenny Jacoby, Pip Tinsley
Picture research Sarah Pownall, Jenny Baskaya
DK picture library Rose Horridge, Myriam Megharbi, Emma Shepherd

Mining
transit

This Eyewitness ® Guide has been conceived by
Dorling Kindersley Limited and Editions Gallimard

First published in Great Britain in 1992.
This revised edition published in 2002, 2008
by Dorling Kindersley Limited, 80 Strand, London WC2R 0RL

ISBN: 978-1-40532-930-9

Colour reproduction by Colourscan, Singapore
Printed and bound by Leo Paper Products Ltd, China

Discover more at
www.dk.com

Lava stalagmite

Figure of Zhang Heng,
Chinese seismologist

Contents

Brown agate

An unstable Earth

VOLCANOES AND EARTHQUAKES are nature run wild. A volcano in eruption may bleed rivers of red-hot lava or spew great clouds of ash and gas into the atmosphere. During a severe earthquake, the solid ground can shake so violently that entire cities are reduced to rubble. These events are disasters that can kill thousands of people. But most volcanoes and earthquakes cause little damage to people or property. They are natural events that happen all over the globe (though in some places more than others). The most familiar volcanoes are graceful, cone-shaped mountains. But any hole through which lava reaches the Earth's surface is a volcano. Some are broad and flat, and most are found deep beneath the sea.

THE PERFECT VOLCANO
The graceful slopes of Mount Fujiyama in Japan rise 3,776 m (12,388 ft) above sea level. This dormant (sleeping) volcano (pp.38–39) is an almost perfect cone. Some Japanese believe that gods live at the summit, which is always shrouded in snow, and often in cloud as well. This view of the peak is one of a set of 36 prints by Katsushika Hokusai (1760–1849).

WALL PAINTING
Nearly 8,000 years old, this wall painting of an eruption of Hassan Dag in Turkey is the earliest known picture of a volcano. The houses of a town, Çatal Hüyük, can be seen at the mountain's foot.

ASH TREATMENT
Eruptions may destroy homes and kill people, but they have their useful side, In Japan, being buried in warm volcanic ash is thought to cure various ailments.

ASHY VOLCANO
Ashy volcanic eruptions (pp.14–15) are unpredictable, and observing them from the ground is dangerous. This false-colour photo of Augustine volcano in Alaska was taken from the safety of a satellite. The ash cloud is being blasted 11km (7 miles) high, through the atmosphere, from where it will be carried far and wide before falling back to Earth.

OLD FAITHFUL
Geysers are springs that spit superheated water and steam high into the air (pp.36–37). They are caused by volcanic heat acting on trapped ground-water. This American geyser, Old Faithful, has erupted every hour for at least 100 years.

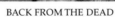

BACK FROM THE DEAD
Most of the people killed or injured in earthquakes are crushed when buildings collapse. This fresco by the 14th-century painter Giotto shows a boy killed in a quake in Assisi, Italy. Legend has it that St Francis of Assisi brought the boy back to life.

SPITTING FIRE
Mount Etna rises 3,390 m (11,122 ft) over the Italian island of Sicily, and is one of the highest mountains and most active volcanoes in Europe. Fountains of gassy lava often spew from the summit (left). Lava flows from a sizeable eruption in 2001 destroyed ski-lift pylons, but stopped short of the village of Nicolisi. The nearby town of Catania is occasionally showered with ash from explosions.

SAN FRANCISCO, 1989
In 1906, San Francisco was flattened by an enormous earthquake. The shaking left large parts of the city in ruins, and the fires that followed added to the destruction. Earthquakes of this size seem to rock the area every hundred years or so. A smaller quake on 17 October, 1989 shook many houses near the waterfront right off their foundations. Some 62 people died in the 15 seconds of shaking.

Fire from below

A JOURNEY TO THE CENTRE OF THE EARTH would produce quite a sweat. Some 200 km (120 miles) down, the temperature is 1,500°C (2,732°F) and the rocks are white hot. Many metals melt long before they get this hot. But because of the intense pressure inside the Earth, the rocks, though soft, are not molten (liquid) until much deeper. Most of the molten rock erupted by volcanoes comes from the top of the mantle, 100 to 300 km (60 to 180 miles) down. Here pockets of magma (molten rock) are produced when the right conditions allow a little melting in between the crystals of the rock. Because magma is hotter and lighter than the surrounding rocks, it rises, melting some of the rocks it passes on the way. If it manages to find a way to the surface, the magma will erupt as lava.

HOT AS HELL
The Irish artist James Barry painted this view of hell in 1788. In the Christian religion, hell is described as a fiery underworld where sinners burn in eternal damnation.

CHANNELS OF FIRE
The centre of the Earth is hard to imagine. In this 17th-century engraving, Athanasius Kircher supposed a fiery core which fed all the volcanoes on the surface. We now know that because of the high pressures, little of the planet's interior is liquid, and there are no subterranean connections between volcanoes.

Red-hot lava (liquid rock) shoots out of a volcano in a curtain of fire

INTO THE CRATER
Jules Verne's famous story *Journey to the Centre of the Earth* begins with a perilous descent into the crater of Mount Etna. After many underground adventures the heroes resurface in a volcanic eruption in Iceland.

THIN-SKINNED
If the Earth was the size of an apple, the tectonic plates (pp.10–13) that cover it would be no thicker than the apple's skin. Like the fruit, the planet has a core. This is surrounded by the mantle – the flesh of the apple.

BASALT
The ocean floors which cover three-quarters of the Earth's surface are made of a dark, heavy volcanic rock called basalt.

GRANITE
The continents are made of a variety of rocks that are mostly lighter in weight and colour than basalt. On average, their composition is similar to granite.

IRON HOT
Pure iron melts when it reaches 1,535°C (2,795°F). Most of the Earth is hotter than this.

Lithosphere, which includes tectonic plates (pp.10–13)

IRON HEART
The iron meteorites that fall to Earth are thought to be pieces of the cores of fragmented planets. Their composition fits in with geophysicists' models of the Earth's metal core.

Inner core of solid metal

Upper mantle

Lower mantle

Outer core of liquid metal

Ultramafic nodule

Ultramafic nodule

INNER SECRETS
No drill hole has yet reached as deep down as the mantle. But occasionally, rising magma tears off fragments of the mantle on its way to the surface. Known as ultramafic nodules, these fragments of very heavy mantle rock are found in erupted lava flows. Their density and chemistry fit in with present geophysical theories about the inside of the Earth.

LAYERS OF EARTH
Beneath the thin, relatively cool rocky crust of Earth lies the mantle. Made of rocky silicates, the mantle is solid, but it generates pockets of magma that feed volcanoes on the surface. Inside the mantle is the Earth's metal core. This consists of an outer core of liquid metal wrapped around a smaller, solid inner core. The pressure here is intense; the metal must be in a very dense form that could not exist at the surface.

CARRYING THE WEIGHT OF THE WORLD
The ancient Romans believed that the
god Atlas held the sky on his shoulders. In
this statue from the first century CE, he is
carrying the entire globe.

The world on a plate

VOLCANOES AND EARTHQUAKES are more common in
some parts of the world than others. This was known
early in the 19th century, but it was not until the
1960s, when the secrets of the deep ocean floor
began to be revealed, that scientists found an
explanation. This became known as the theory of
plate tectonics ("tectonic" is a Greek word that
means building). The tectonic theory says that the
Earth's surface is fragmented into pieces which
fit together like odd-shaped paving stones. Called
tectonic plates, these chunks of the Earth's skin
move across its surface in response to forces and
movements deep within the planet. The plate
boundaries, where plates collide, rub together,
or move apart, are areas of intense geological
activity. Most volcanoes and earthquakes
occur at these boundaries, and the nature
of the boundary dictates the nature of the
volcanoes and earthquakes
that occur there.

CONTINENTAL DRIFTER

A German meteorologist, Alfred
Wegener (1880–1930) coined the term
"continental drift". He saw the fit of
the coastlines of South America
and Africa, and their similarities
in terms of geology and fossils,
and suggested that they had
once been attached. However,
at the time there was no
known way that the continents could have moved apart. For more
than half a century his ideas were largely ignored by geophysicists.
Only when spreading ridges (pp.24–25) were discovered 40 years
later was his theory accepted.

RING OF FIRE

More than 1,500 active volcanoes on Earth rise above sea level, and
every year there are over a million earthquakes, mostly tiny tremors too
small to be felt. In this map, the black cones are volcanoes and the red
zones are prone to earthquakes. Both are common along the "Ring of
Fire", the edges of the plates that form the floor of the Pacific Ocean.

LESSONS OF HISTORY

This plaster cast shows a man killed in the eruption of Mount Vesuvius which devastated the Roman towns of Pompeii and Herculaneum in 79 CE (pp.26–31). Contemporary accounts and the more recent excavations still tell the horrific story of the eruption.

LIVING ON THE RING OF FIRE

There are more than 70 active volcanoes in Japan, and few weeks go by without an earthquake or two. This huge quake in 1925 damaged the historic city of Kyoto.

Like Japan, Kamchatka is part of the Pacific Ring of Fire

Alaska and the Aleutian Islands have many volcanoes and earthquakes

Iceland sits on top of the Mid-Atlantic spreading ridge (pp.24–25)

The Mid-Atlantic Ridge is part of the largest mountain range in the world

The island of Reunion was formed by a hot spot (pp.22–23) that was under India 30 million years ago

Antarctica is surrounded by new ocean made by spreading ridges (pp.24–25)

Indonesia, home to over 125 active volcanoes, is at the boundary of two plates

DRIFTING PLATES

This globe has been coloured to highlight the tectonic plates. One plate may contain both continent and ocean crust. The Australian Plate, for instance, includes a large part of the Indian Ocean. It is thus the plates, and not the continents, that are on the move.

There are no active volcanoes in Australia, which sits in the middle of a plate

Mount Erebus, an active volcano in Antarctica

11

Continued on next page

FIRELAND
Iceland might better
be called Fireland,
as it is a land of
volcanoes and
geysers. The island is
made almost entirely
of volcanic rocks like
those found on the
deep ocean floor. It
has gradually built
up above sea level
through intense and
prolonged eruptions.

Moving plates

Wherever tectonic plates meet, the great stresses of the jostling rocks
are released in earthquakes. Most volcanoes also occur at plate
boundaries, where melting rock forms magma that erupts at the
surface. When two plates move apart, a spreading ridge – a chain
of gentle volcanoes – is formed. Where plates collide, one is forced
beneath the other to form a subduction zone. The sinking plate partly
melts and the hot liquid magma rises to feed volcanoes just inside
the plate boundary. A third kind of volcano erupts above a hot spot,
an active centre in the Earth's mantle.

*Ocean floor is older
the farther it is
from the ridge*

*Rift where ocean
floor is pulled
apart*

*Old volcanoes that have
moved away from hot spot*

*Hot spot volcano, builds up
a mountain so large it
forms an island*

50
km

100 km

*Magma erupts in the
rift as pulled-apart
plates release pressure*

*Hot plume of magma
rises to form a hot spot*

*The new plate cools and
thickens as it moves away
from the heat of the ridge*

SPREADING RIDGES
New ocean floor is made where plates are pulled apart
(pp.24–25), creating a down-faulted rift. Here magma
rises and erupts as lava through fissures and vents.
Continued rifting produces successive new rifts and
separates the parallel, flanking ridges – each one older
than the next. All the ocean floor has been made this
way in the last 200 million years.

HOT SPOTS
Hot spot volcanoes (pp.22–23) are not found at
plate margins. They are caused by active centres in
the mantle which produce huge volumes of magma.
The magma rises to the surface and punches a hole
in the plate, forming a volcano. Because the hot spot
in the mantle stays still while the plate moves over
it, the hot spot seems to drift across the plate.

VOLCANO CHAIN
Guatemala in Central America is home to a chain of volcanoes, many still active. They sit on top of a subduction zone formed as the Cocos Plate sinks beneath the larger North American Plate.

AMERICA'S FAULT
The San Andreas fault zone is probably the most famous plate boundary in the world. It is easy to see the direction of movement from rivers and roads, even whole mountain ranges that have been split apart by the relentless sideways sliding.

A deep ocean trench is formed where the ocean floor descends in a subduction zone

Continental margin thickened and lifted above subduction zone

There are few volcanoes along transcurrent plate margins

Ocean plate heated as it plunges into the mantle

Lightest melted rock rises through the surrounding dense rocks

Magma reservoir feeds volcano

Lithosphere (crust and very top of mantle)

Asthenosphere (soft, upper part of mantle)

SUBDUCTION ZONE
Where one plate is pushed below another, it descends into the mantle along a subduction zone. As the plates grind past one another, earthquakes are generated, some very large. At depth, the friction melts some rocks to form magma. This liquid magma rises to feed volcanoes within the margin of the plate above (pp.14–15).

RUBBING SHOULDERS
A transcurrent plate margin is formed where two plates meet at an odd angle. The resulting boundary is called a transcurrent fault zone. Large earthquakes occur when the fault sticks, then suddenly slips.

When a mountain explodes

SLUMBERING GIANT
Before the cataclysmic events of May 1980, Mount St Helens was a mountain wonderland visited by tourists who found tranquillity in its forests and lakes.

THE MOST SPECTACULAR AND DESTRUCTIVE eruptions occur at volcanoes by subduction zones (pp.10–13). These volcanoes may lie dormant for many centuries between eruptions (pp.38–39). When they do explode, the eruption can be extraordinarily violent. When Mount St Helens, a volcano in the Cascade range in northwest USA, blew its top on 18 May, 1980, it had been quiet for 123 years. The huge explosion that decapitated the mountain was heard in Vancouver, Canada, 320 km (200 miles) to the north. The north side of the mountain was pulverised and blown out over the surrounding forest. This avalanche of rock was quickly overtaken by clouds of newly erupted ash. These became pyroclastic flows (p.16), flows of hot ash and gas that rushed down the steep slopes of the volcano at terrifying speeds, incinerating everything they met. The explosion continued for nine hours, lofting millions of tonnes of ash 22 km (15 miles) up into the atmosphere. Mud flows choked the river valleys with a mixture of ash, ice, and uprooted trees (pp.56–57). Vast areas of forest were flattened by the blast and 57 people, including the volcanologist David Johnston, were killed.

38 SECONDS AFTER THE FIRST EXPLOSION
After two months of small earthquakes and explosions, the north slope of Mount St Helens had grown a huge bulge. At 8.32 in the morning of 18 May, the whole north side suddenly shivered and seemed to turn to liquid. As the pressure inside the volcano was reduced, the hot magma down below began to froth and explode. This picture, taken 38 seconds into the explosion, shows the avalanche roaring down the north face. Just above the avalanche, a cloud of ash and gas is blasting skywards.

Ashy eruption cloud

Feeder pipe

Reservoir of hot, gassy magma

FEEDING THE FURY
Lighter than the solid rock around it, hot magma had risen under Mount St Helens. The magma was melt from old oceanic plate consumed in the subduction zone off the coast (pp.12–13). It had gathered in an underground pool, the magma reservoir. The hot rock reached the crater along a feeder pipe, which took on the shape of a gun barrel as the eruption progressed.

FOUR SECONDS LATER...
...the avalanche of old rock has been overtaken by the darker, growing cloud of ash, which contains newly erupted material. Gary Rosenquist who took these pictures said later that "the sight... was so overwhelming that I became dizzy and had to turn away to keep my balance". From his viewpoint 18 km (11 miles) away, he didn't hear a sound through the whole blast.

MOVING WALL OF ASH
As the ash cloud blasted out beyond the flanks of the volcano, it became lighter than air and began to rise. Gary Rosenquist took this last picture before he ran for his car. "The turbulent cloud loomed behind us as we sped down Road 99," he wrote later. "We raced toward Randle as marble-sized mudballs flattened against the windshield. Minutes later it was completely dark. We groped through the choking ash cloud to safety."

LAST GASP
In the months after the big eruption, the diminishing pressure in the magma reservoir pushed up thick, pasty lava. The sticky rock was squeezed out like toothpaste from a tube. It formed a bulging dome, which reached a height of 260 m (800 ft) in 1986. At one point, a spine of stiff lava grew out of the dome. Like the bigger spine pushed up by Mount Pelée in 1902 (pp.32–33), this eventually crumbled to a heap of lava fragments.

TREE-REMOVAL ZONE
Mature forests of trees up to 50 m (150 ft) tall were flattened by the blast of the eruption. Closest to the mountain, in the "tree-removal zone", the ground was scoured of virtually everything.

ELEVEN SECONDS LATER...
... the avalanche of old rock has been completely overtaken by the faster blast of ash. On the right, huge chunks of airborne rock can be clearly seen as they are catapulted out of the cloud.

Ash and dust

Lapilli, bite-sized fragments of frothy lava

Ash, smaller pyroclastic fragments

Dust, the smallest, lightest lava fragments

THE MOST EXPLOSIVE VOLCANOES pour clouds of ash high into the sky. The ash is formed because gas dissolved in the magma escapes with such force that it blasts the hot rock into billions of tiny pieces. The resulting rock fragments are collectively known as pyroclastics. They range from lava blocks as big as houses (p.18) to powdery dust fine enough to float right around the world in the upper atmosphere (pp.34–35). Between these two extremes are lapilli (Latin for "little stones") and ash. Very powerful explosive eruptions can hurl huge blocks several kilometres from the volcano. But the biggest fragments usually land nearest to the vent, while the smallest ones are flung the farthest. In some eruptions, the ash clouds collapse under their own weight, forming pyroclastic flows. Unlike lava flows, pyroclastic flows can be extremely dangerous. Many of the worst volcanic disasters have been caused by pyroclastic flows or pyroclastic surges, flows containing more hot gas than ash.

CONSTRUCTING A CONE
Mountains are built up as pyroclastics burst from the crater and settle layer upon layer on a volcano's slopes. Gassy fire-fountain eruptions build cinder cones of bombs and ash. These cinder cones are two of several in a crater in Maui, Hawaii (pp.22–23).

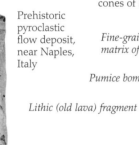

Prehistoric pyroclastic flow deposit, near Naples, Italy

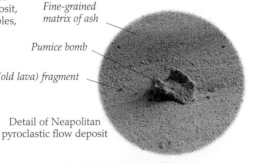

Fine-grained matrix of ash

Pumice bomb

Lithic (old lava) fragment

Detail of Neapolitan pyroclastic flow deposit

GLOWING AVALANCHES
If the erupted mixture of hot rocks and gas is heavier than air, it may flow downhill at more than 100 kph (60 mph). Such a pyroclastic flow (also called an ash flow, *nuée ardente*, or glowing avalanche) may flatten everything in its path. Equally destructive are pyroclastic surges, flows that contain more hot gas than ash. The residents of Pompeii (pp.26–30) and St Pierre (pp.32–33) were killed by searing pyroclastic surges.

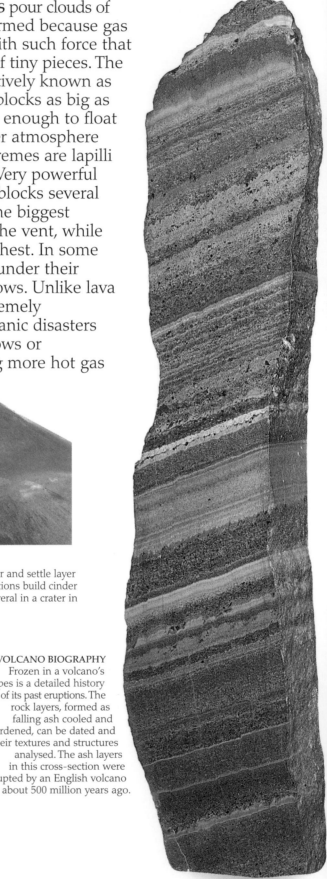

VOLCANO BIOGRAPHY
Frozen in a volcano's slopes is a detailed history of its past eruptions. The rock layers, formed as falling ash cooled and hardened, can be dated and their textures and structures analysed. The ash layers in this cross-section were erupted by an English volcano about 500 million years ago.

Their fields buried in ash, farmers take their buffaloes and head for greener pastures

Long night of the ash cloud

After lying dormant for 600 years, Mount Pinatubo in the Philippines began erupting in June 1991. Huge clouds of ash were thrown into the air, blocking out the sunlight for days. The airborne ash slowly settled out, burying fields and villages for kilometres around. Over 100 m (330 ft) of ash lay in drifts on the upper slopes of the volcano. Torrential rains followed, causing mud flows that cascaded down the river valleys and swept away roads, bridges, and several villages (p.56). At least 400 people were killed and another 400,000 were left homeless. With no breathing masks to protect themselves from the gritty ash, many of the survivors developed pneumonia. At the very least, their eyes were badly inflamed by the ashy air.

BURIED CROPS
A thin fall of ash fertilises the soil (pp.40–41), but too much destroys crops. With no water to wash off the abrasive powder, this maize is inedible. Whole harvests were lost in the heavy ash falls that followed the eruptions of Mount Pinatubo.

BREATHING EASY
Every step raises fine ash which fills the air. Covering mouth and nose with a wet cloth helps to keep the throat and lungs clear.

Fiery rocks

VOLCANOES ERUPT red-hot lava. Sometimes the lava oozes gently from a hole in the ground. At other times it is thrown into the air in spectacular fire fountains, running together again as it lands. Either way, the lava flows off in rivers of hot rock that may spread out and cover the countryside before it cools. Fire fountains and lava flows are common in Iceland (pp.24–25) and Hawaii (pp.22–23). They are relatively predictable, and it's often possible to venture near them and photograph them in close-up. But if the lava is less fluid and its supply is variable, explosions occur from time to time as volcanic gas escapes from the hot rock. As the gas content changes, a volcano may switch without warning from one type of eruption to another. Explosions throw out bombs and blocks, chunks of flying lava that litter the ground around the vent. It is dangerous to get close to explosive eruptions because the size and timing of the explosions varies.

REMELTED LAVA
Some of the gas dissolved in lava is lost when it erupts and cools. This piece of once-cold lava was reheated and remelted in a special oven. It frothed up a lot, showing that it still contained a lot of its original gas.

A red iron oxide covers this bomb thrown out by Mount Etna, on the island of Sicily in Italy (pp.6–7)

Dense round bomb

BOMBS AND BLOCKS
Bombs and blocks can be as big as houses or as small as tennis balls. Bombs are usually more rounded, while blocks are more dense and angular. Their shapes depend upon how molten or gassy the lava was during flight. Very liquid chunks of lava plop to the ground like cow pats; denser, more solid ones thud or shatter as they land. Both bombs and blocks draw long, fiery traces when they are photographed at night with a long time exposure.

Small, explosive eruption photographed at night on Mount Etna

A TWISTED TAIL
The odd twists and tails of many bombs are formed as they spin through the air.

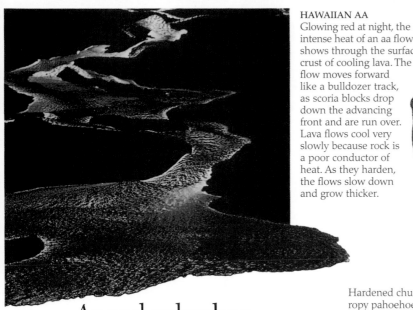

HAWAIIAN AA
Glowing red at night, the intense heat of an aa flow shows through the surface crust of cooling lava. The flow moves forward like a bulldozer track, as scoria blocks drop down the advancing front and are run over. Lava flows cool very slowly because rock is a poor conductor of heat. As they harden, the flows slow down and grow thicker.

Hardened chunk of ropy pahoehoe lava

PAHOEHOE FLOWS
Pahoehoe is more fluid than aa and contains more gas. As its surface cools, the flow grows a thin, pliable skin. The hot lava on the inside distorts the skin, wrinkling it so its surface looks like the coils of a rope. The crust may grow so thick that people can walk across it while red-hot lava continues to flow in a tunnel below (p.23). The hot lava may remelt the overlying crust, which drips off. Kept hot by tunnels, pahoehoe lava can flow as far as villages on the volcano's lower slopes.

Aa and pahoehoe

Lava flows pose little danger to people as they rarely travel faster than a few kilometres an hour. The two kinds of flows get their names from Hawaiian words. Aa (pronounced *ah-ah*) flows are covered in sharp, angular chunks of lava known as scoria. This makes them difficult to walk over when they have cooled, unlike pahoehoe (*pa-hoy-hoy*) flows, which grow a smooth skin soon after they leave the vent. The chilled surface traps gas, keeping flows hot and mobile. Pahoehoe flows are rarely more than 1 m (3 ft) thick, while the thickest aa flows may be 100 m (330 ft) high.

Driblets of remelted lava from the roof of a pahoehoe tunnel

SPINY AND TWISTED
This chunk of scoria from the surface of an aa flow was twisted as it was carried along.

PAHOEHOE TOE
This picture shows red-hot pahoehoe bulging through a crack in its own skin. New skin is forming over the bulge. A pahoehoe flow creeps forward with thousands of little breakouts like this one.

FIRE AND WATER
Volcanic islands like Hawaii and Iceland are usually fringed by black beaches. The sand is formed when hot lava hits the sea and is shattered into tiny, glassy particles. It is black because the lava is rich in dark minerals like iron oxides and low in light-coloured ones like quartz.

Black sand from the volcanic island of Santorini in Greece

Gas and lightning

VOLCANIC GASES ARE EXTREMELY DANGEROUS. In August 1986, a small explosion in Lake Nyos in Cameroon, Central Africa, signalled the release of a cloud of volcanic gases. The poisonous fumes killed 1,700 people living in villages below the lake. The main killer in the cloud was carbon dioxide, a heavy gas which flows downhill and gathers in hollows.

Captain Haddock and friends flee from a volcano's sulphurous gases in the Tintin adventure *Flight 71.4. for Sydney*

Carbon dioxide is particularly dangerous because it has no odour and is very hard to detect - unlike many volcanic gases, which are extremely smelly. Hydrogen sulphide smells like rotten cabbage, and the acid gases hydrogen chloride and sulphur dioxide prick the eyes and throat. They also eat through clothes, leaving holes with bleached haloes around them. Hydrogen fluoride, which is very poisonous, is strong enough to etch glass. Early volcano observers who thought they saw flames during eruptions were probably looking at great veils of glowing gases. Flames occur when hydrogen gas catches fire, but they are flimsy and hard to see. More impressive are lightning flashes, which are often seen during ashy eruptions.

RAISING A STINK
Nearly 40 years after the last eruption of Kawah Idjen in Java, Indonesia, sulphur and other gases are still escaping into the volcano's crater. Here volcanologist Katia Krafft (pp.42–43) collects gas samples from the crater floor.

STEAM-ASSISTED ERUPTION
Water expands enormously when it turns to steam. So when magma meets water, the power of the eruption is orders of magnitude greater. When the new island of Surtsey was formed off Iceland in November 1963 (p.41), sea water poured into the vent and hit the hot magma, producing spectacular explosions and huge clouds of steam.

GAS MASK
Made to protect the wearer against low concentrations of acid gases, this gas mask also keeps out all but the finest volcanic dust.

Volcanologist studying Hawaiian lava flows behind the safety of a gas mask

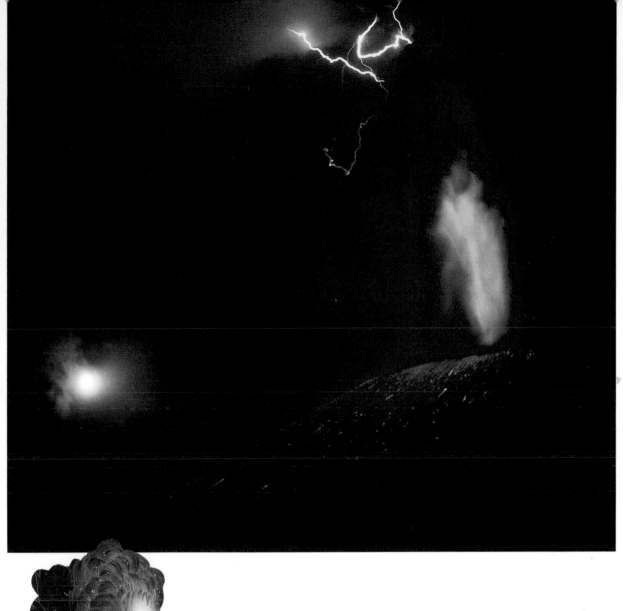

LIGHTNING FLASH
Immense flashes of lightning are often seen during eruptions. They are caused by a build-up of static electricity produced when the tiny fragments of lava in an ash cloud rub against each other. The electrical charge is released in bolts that leap through the cloud, as they do in a thunderstorm. This picture shows lightning bolts at Mount Tolbachik in Kamchatka, Siberia. It was taken during the day - the Sun can be seen on the far left, shining feebly through a cloud of dust and gas.

VESUVIUS FLASHES
British ambassador to Naples Lord Hamilton saw lightning flashes as he watched the 1779 eruption of Mount Vesuvius (p.31).

FLOATING ON AN ACID LAKE
Volcanologists sample volcanic gases on the surface of an acid lake in the crater of Kawah Idjen. The gases rising from the volcano are dissolved in the lake water which fills much of the crater. Such acid lakes are very hostile to life, and would devour a swimmer's skin in minutes.

FLOATING ROCK
The volcanic rock pumice is light because it is full of bubbles of gas. If it contains enough bubbles, it becomes light enough to float on water.

Hot spots

THE LARGEST VOLCANOES ON EARTH are above hot spots. Two of the biggest, Mauna Loa and Kilauea, are on the island of Hawaii. The Hawaiian island chain is the tip of a huge undersea mountain range that has built up over millions of years as the hot spot erupted great volumes of lava onto the moving plate above it. Hot spots are randomly distributed, and have little if any relation to today's plate boundaries (pp.12–15). Some geologists believe that certain hot spots relate to old plate boundary positions. Fractures which were part of the old boundary system still act as channels for magma to escape to the surface. This reduces the pressure on the mantle, which in turn stimulates further melting, making more magma to feed the hot spot. Other hot spots may be initiators of new plate boundaries. Iceland is a hot spot 2,000 km (1,200 miles) across. If it weren't for this huge volcanic structure buoying it up, much of northwest Europe would be below sea level.

VOLCANO GODDESS
Some Hawaiians believe that the powerful goddess Pele makes mountains, melts rocks, destroys forests, and builds new islands. The fiery goddess is said to live in the crater Halema'uma'u, at the summit of Kilauea volcano on the island of Hawaii.

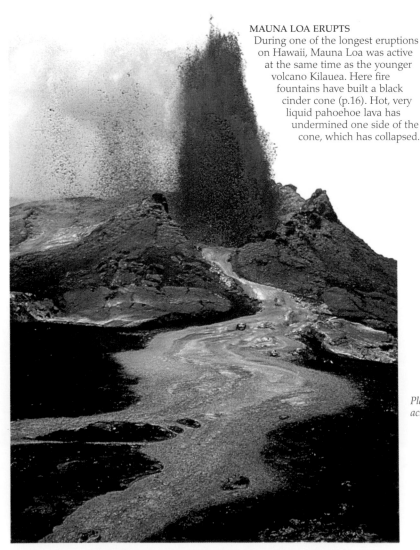

MAUNA LOA ERUPTS
During one of the longest eruptions on Hawaii, Mauna Loa was active at the same time as the younger volcano Kilauea. Here fire fountains have built a black cinder cone (p.16). Hot, very liquid pahoehoe lava has undermined one side of the cone, which has collapsed.

Kauai

Oahu

Maui

Hawaii

Plate moving across hot spot

Stationary hot spot

A STRING OF ISLANDS
The Pacific Plate is moving over the stationary Hawaiian hot spot, which is presently under the south end of the island of Hawaii. There are two active volcanoes, Mauna Loa and Kilauea, on Hawaii, and a third, Loihi, is growing below the sea to the south. The north end of the island of Hawaii is made up of older, extinct volcanoes, and a string of progressively older volcanic islands lies to the northwest.

PELE'S HAIR
The hot, fluid lava of a Hawaiian fire fountain may be blown into fine, glassy strands. These are known as Pele's hair.

WANDERING HOT SPOT
Hot-spot volcanoes erupt often and are relatively easy to get close to and photograph. This is Piton de la Fournaise on the island of Réunion in the Indian Ocean (p.11). The island is the tip of a huge volcano that rises 7 km (4 miles) above the ocean floor. The hot spot has moved 4,000 km (2,500 miles) in the last 30 million years.

Lava has solidified around this tree, leaving a tree mould

Road buried by lava during eruption of Kilauea

UP IN FLAMES
Lava in tubes remains hot and fluid, so it can travel many kilometres from the vent, engulfing fertile land and villages on the way.

LAVA TUBE
The skin of a pahoehoe flow may crust over into a roof thick enough to walk on. Only a metre or so below, hot lava continues to run in a tunnel or "tube". Occasional collapses in the roof provide a window through which the flowing lava can be watched and measured. Hot lava dripping off the underside of the roof creates strange formations called lava stalagmites and stalactites.

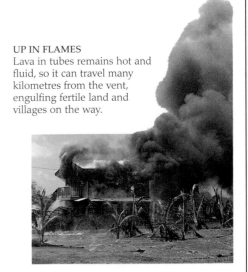

Lava stalagmite made of drips in a pahoehoe tube

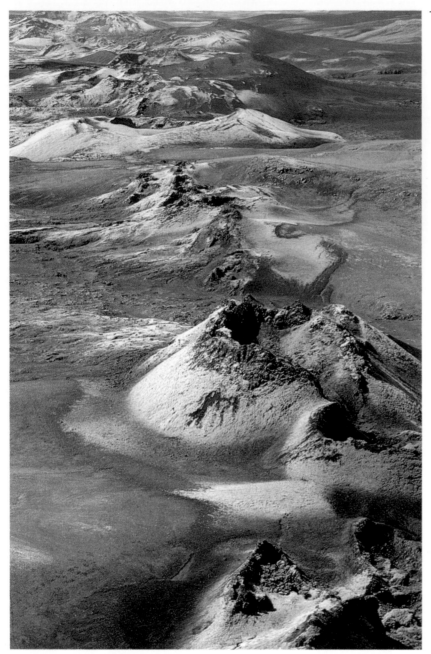

Spreading ridges

THE ROCKS THAT MAKE up the ocean floor are all young – nowhere older than 200 million years. This is because new ocean plate is constantly being made by volcanic eruptions deep below the ocean waters. A long range of mountains snakes through the oceans, cut at its heart by a rift valley. The volcanoes in this rift valley erupt constantly, producing new volcanic rock. Under the huge pressure of the ocean water, the lava erupts gently, like toothpaste squeezed from a tube, to form rounded shapes known as pillow lava. The new rock fills in the widening rift as the plates pull apart. In this way the oceans grow just a little wider, a centimetre or so a year. In places, the rifts are bubbling with volcanic hot springs – black smokers – that exude water rich in metal sulphides. First discovered in 1977, black smokers are the subject of intense research. They are home to lifeforms found nowhere else on the planet.

RIFT THROUGH ICELAND
In Iceland, geologists can study ridges without getting wet. This is the Skaftar fissure, part of a 27-km (16-mile) long rift that opened in 1783, erupting 13 cubic km (3.1 cubic miles) of lava over eight months. The dust and gas killed 75 per cent of the animals in Iceland, and 10,000 Icelanders died in the famine that followed.

UNDERSEA VOLCANO
A long-range side-scan sonar known as GLORIA created this image of a volcano 4,000 m (13,000 ft) below the Pacific Ocean. The submarine volcano is 10 km (6 miles) across.

Icelandic eruptions give a glimpse of how spreading ridges make new oceanic plate. The eruptions tend to be from long cracks, rather than central craters.

Africa   *Red Sea*   *Arabia*

SPLITTING CONTINENT
A spreading ridge runs through the Red Sea. For the last 20 million years it has been making new ocean floor, as Arabia moves away from Africa.

Submersible *Alvin*, which took photos of mid-ocean ridges

Rounded pillow shapes typical of lava erupted underwater

Black smokers

These hot springs are found along spreading ridges in spots where the ridges are particularly active. The water they pour forth is hot, acidic, and black with sulphides of copper, lead, and zinc. These valuable metal minerals come from the new oceanic plate that is formed at the ridges. They are dissolved out by sea water percolating through the cooling rock.

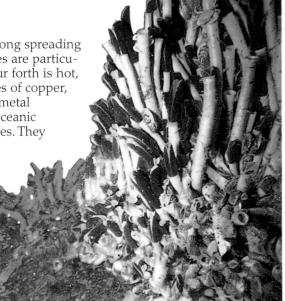

Sulphur-eating tube worms from the Galapagos rift

MANGANESE NODULES
The ocean floor is carpeted with black lumps rich in manganese and other metals. If a way of collecting them from deep water can be found, these nodules may become a valuable source of minerals.

LIVING WITHOUT SUNLIGHT
The many strange lifeforms found around black smokers live off microbes that, in turn, are nourished by mineral-eating microbes. These urchins were seen on the Galapagos rift.

Plume of black metal sulphides   *Black smoker chimney*

Feeder channel or pipe

Cold sea water percolating through hot rock

Model of black smoker

Magma reservoir

LAVA FEEDER CHANNELS
Two ancient lava feeder channels can be seen in the rock above.

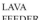

Coarse crystal structure indicates slow cooling

CHIMNEY PIPES
Chilled suddenly as they meet cold ocean water, the metal sulphides crystallise out to form the chimney pipes that surround the mouths of black smokers. These grow steadily, collapsing only when they get too tall.

Gabbro, a coarsely crystalline rock from an old seafloor magma reservoir in Cyprus

The great eruption of Vesuvius

PLINY THE YOUNGER
This scholar watched the eruption cloud from across the Bay of Naples, where he was staying with his uncle, Pliny the Elder.

Perhaps the most famous eruption of all time shook Mount Vesuvius near Naples in Italy in 79 CE. When the long-dormant volcano erupted on 24 August, the residents of the Roman towns of Pompeii and Herculaneum were caught unawares. Hot ash and lapilli rained down on Pompeii for hours until it was buried several metres deep. Many people escaped, coughing and stumbling through the darkness of the ash cloud. Those caught in the town were overwhelmed by a sudden powerful blast of ash and gas (a pyroclastic surge, p.16). The apocalyptic events were described in detail by Pliny the Younger. His famous letters to Tacitus are the first known eyewitness account of a volcanic eruption. The buried towns were virtually forgotten until excavations began in the 18th century. The digs have since unearthed a priceless archeological and geological treasure, two thriving Roman towns frozen in the moments of their destruction.

Solfatara Volcano · Naples · Mount Vesuvius · Herculaneum · Pompeii · Castellammare · Ash cloud

BLOWING IN THE WIND
The wind blew Vesuvius' ash cloud south onto the town of Pompeii. Herculaneum, to the west of the volcano, was hardly touched by falling ash. But the pyroclastic flows and surges (p.16) that followed flowed downhill in all directions, covering both towns.

BURNT TO A TOAST
This carbonised loaf of bread was one of several found in the brick oven of a bakery. The baker's stamp can still be seen, nearly 2,000 years after the day the bread was baked.

Modern Italian bread

BEWARE OF DOG
This floor mosaic from a Pompeii entranceway was meant to warn off intruders. A similar mosaic says *cave canem* – Latin for "beware of the dog".

Flour mill made of lava, a tough rock also used to pave streets

Portrait of a poetess or princess, detail of a floor mosaic found at Pompeii

Bowl of preserved eggs

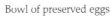

SNAKE CHARM
Fine gold and silver jewellery, some set with emeralds, was found in the buried town. This hollow bracelet in the shape of a coiled snake is made of thick gold. Certain styles were abundant. Over 80 copies of one kind of earring were found, suggesting mass production of popular models.

Fresh walnuts

Fresh figs, still grown on the slopes of Vesuvius

Bowl of carbonised figs

Carbonised food
Organic compounds like wood, bone, and food contain carbon. Normally they would burn when heated. But in some circumstances, the hot ash and gas stopped oxygen from combining with the carbon, so that the compounds turned to charcoal instead. This process, called carbonisation, left the fine details of many foodstuffs perfectly preserved in the fine ash.

Bowl of carbonised walnuts

PANIC IN THE STREETS
The large theatre (the open, semi-circular building) and the gladiator's gymnasium (in front of the theatre) can be seen in this artist's impression of the destruction of Pompeii. In the crowded streets, stragglers are running for their lives from the menacing black clouds.

DEATH OF PLINY THE ELDER
In one letter, Pliny the Younger wrote of his uncle and another official fleeing with "pillows tied upon their heads with napkins; and this was their whole defence against the storm of stones that fell around them. It was now day everywhere else, but there a deeper darkness prevailed than in the thickest night…my uncle … raised himself up with the assistance of two of his servants, and instantly fell down dead; suffocated, as I conjecture, by some gross and noxious vapour… his body was found entire… looking more like a man asleep than dead."

Continued on next page

Continued from previous page

THE FAITHFUL DOG
This guard dog found at the house of Vesonius Primus died at his post, still tethered by a chain attached to his bronze collar.

Caught in the act of dying

Over 2,000 people died in Pompeii when the eruption of Mount Vesuvius overwhelmed the Roman town. We know about these Roman citizens from plaster casts that show them at the moment of their death. As the fleeing Pompeiians died, the rain of ash and pumice set around their bodies rather like wet cement. With time, the soft body parts decayed and the ash and pumice turned to solid rock. The shapes of the dead Romans' bodies were left as hollows in the rock. Only the hard bones remained inside the hollows. In 1860, the Italian king appointed Giuseppe Fiorelli as director of the excavations. Fiorelli started the first systematic, large-scale excavations of the ancient city. He also invented a method for removing the skeletons from the body hollows and filling the space with wet plaster of Paris. After the plaster hardened, a true representation of the bodies could be dug out of the volcanic rock. Many of these startling casts show people grimacing, trying to hide, or huddling together in terror. Excavations at Pompeii continue today, and Fiorelli's method is still used whenever new bodies are unearthed. It has also been used to make casts of animals, trees, doors, furniture, and cart wheels.

Body cavity is discovered

Cavity is filled with wet plaster of Paris

LAST DAY OF POMPEII
Fascinated by the apocalyptic stories of Pompeii, many artists have depicted its destruction. Like most, this painting by 19th-century German artist Karl Bruillov is rather fanciful. He has shown flames as houses catch fire.

Cast of suffocated baby, found in the Garden of the Fugitives

SHROUD OF DEATH
His body cast shows the folds of the clothing this man was wearing when he died. He is clutching his chest, indicating his pain in breathing. Most of the victims are believed to have died of suffocation.

Cast of man who died
shielting his face with his hands

*Part of
woman's
skull shows
through cast*

**KILLED
ON DUTY**
When the
American writer
Mark Twain visited
Pompeii, he was most
impressed by the remains of
a soldier who had stayed
at his post "till the hell
that raged around him
burned out the
dauntless spirit it
could not
conquer."

MOTHER AND CHILD
This mother was trying to
shield her child when they were
overcome by the searing ash and
gas. They were found together
with several other families in the
Garden of the Fugitives.

HEALTH WARNING
This skeleton mosaic found
near Pompeii is a memento mori, a reminder of
death. The figure is carrying wine jugs, perhaps
to warn Romans of the dangers of drinking.

Fiorelli takes detailed notes while
supervising an excavation

*Pyroclastic
flow deposit*
*Pyroclastic
surge deposits*
Ash and lapilli

ROCK LAYERS
Pompeii was
buried by 2 m
(6 ft) of ash and
lapilli, then two
pyroclastic
surges and a
large flow.

29

Continued on next page

Continued from previous page

Herculaneum

In 79 CE, the Roman town of Herculaneum was a luxurious seaside resort. When Mount Vesuvius began to erupt on 24 August, the great ash cloud that engulfed Pompeii missed Herculaneum (p.26). Less than 3 cm (1 in) of debris had fallen on the town when it was blasted by a great surge of hot ash and gas. Early excavations uncovered very few bodies, which was puzzling. Archeologists decided that most of the inhabitants must have escaped in boats before the surge. But in the 1980s, several hundred skeletons were found huddled beneath massive brick arches that once stood on the shoreline. A great crowd of Herculaneans must have taken shelter there, only to be overcome by the deadly waves of ash and gas.

NEPTUNE AND AMPHITRITE
This mosaic of two mythological figures was unearthed in the courtyard of a wealthy wine merchant's house in Herculaneum.

WALKING IN THE RUINS
The excavations of the Roman town have created a deep hole that is surrounded by the modern city of Herculaneum (p.60). These visitors to the ruins are walking on a street laid with lava paving stones.

ROMAN SKELETONS
Unlike the bones found in Pompeii, the skeletons from Herculaneum have no surrounding body shape. This is because the ground they lay in was waterlogged. As the bodies decayed, the wet ash nestled closer and closer until it was packed tightly around the bones.

A TOMB OF HOT ROCK
Herculaneum was hit by six pyroclastic surges (p.16–17). Each one was followed by a thick flow of hot ash, pumice, and rock. The flows buried the town in 20 m (65 ft) of volcanic debris – five times more than covered the neighbouring town of Pompeii.

TEXT BOOK ERUPTION
This 1767 engraving (above), which probably shows the 1760 eruption, was published in Millar's *New Complete & Universal System of Geography*.

1631 eruption (left)

HAMILTON'S VIEW
The British ambassador to Naples, Lord Hamilton (p.21), included this view of the 1779 eruption in his book *The Campi Phlegraei* (which literally means "flaming fields"). The artist is Pietro Fabris (p.39).

The world's most visited volcano

The Romans who lived in the shadow of Vesuvius were scarcely aware that it was a volcano. The mountain had erupted 800 years earlier, but it had been calm since and its slopes had grown green and tranquil. Vesuvius was more explosive after 79 CE, erupting numerous times in the 20 centuries since Pompeii and Herculaneum were destroyed. The biggest recent eruption, in 1631, produced pyroclastic surges and flows. Since the 18th century, travellers have flocked to Naples to see the excavations, the art treasures, and the angry mountain. Even today tourists make the difficult climb to the summit and pay to look into the steaming crater.

German etching of 1885 eruption showing fires started by lava flows

ON THE TOURIST MAP
This satirical cartoon shows English tourists at the crater of Vesuvius in 1890. A tourist guide-book of 1883 warns visitors that all guides are impostors. It advises sightseers to wear their worst clothes because boots are ruined by the sharp lava and colourful dresses are stained by the sulphur.

Vesuv. Ash rain of the eruption (March 1944: days 22. 23. 24. 25. 26)

TRAVELLING IN STYLE
From 1890 to 1944, a funicular railway carried sightseers up to the crater of Vesuvius. Here tourists watch the 1933 eruption.

SOUVENIR OF VESUVIUS
Centuries ago, souvenirs from Naples included Roman artefacts stolen from the excavations. These days security is tighter, and boxes of lava and ash are more common souvenirs. Guide books should warn that some of the boxes contain colourful industrial slag instead!

A modern Pompeii: St Pierre

ONE OF THE WORST VOLCANIC DISASTERS of the 20th century happened on 8 May, 1902 on the French Caribbean island of Martinique. It was Ascension Day, and most of the inhabitants of St Pierre were ignoring Mount Pelée, the volcano that towered over the city. When it erupted, just before 8 a.m., the mountain sent a cloud of glowing gas down upon the picturesque port. St Pierre and all its inhabitants were engulfed. Eyewitnesses on ships in the harbour described the cloud as shrivelling and incinerating everything it touched. One said "the wave of fire was on us and over us like a lightning flash. It sounded like thousands of cannon." Within minutes, St Pierre was charred beyond recognition. The blasted remains bore only a thin coating of ash as witness to the horrific cloud. A few sailors survived on their ships, but all but two of the city's 29,000 residents were killed.

SCARRED SURVIVOR
The heat pitted the surface of this statue. Like many objects, it shows more intense heating on the side facing the volcano – in this case the far side.

ALFRED LACROIX
French volcanologist Alfred Lacroix arrived in St Pierre on June 23 and spent a year studying Mount Pelée. In his famous report on the eruption, he described the strange *nuées ardentes* or "glowing clouds" that overran St Pierre. Nowadays these would be called pyroclastic flows or surges (p.16).

Broken statuette

WHEN THE CLOCKS STOPPED
This pocket watch was melted to a standstill at 8:15 a.m.

Melted medicine bottle

Carbonised spaghetti

Carbonised prune

Ash fragment

Remains of mousetrap

MELTED GLASS
Like the excavations of Pompeii, the ruins of St Pierre still give up the secrets of the awful event. Discovered in the 1950s, these partially melted objects bear witness to everyday life in a small French colony at the beginning of the 20th century. Some are either so melted or so unfamiliar that it is hard to guess what they are.

Fine volcanic ash melted into glaze

Melted wine bottle

Melted metal fork (rust occurred after eruption)

Top of charred human
femur (thigh bone)

RUINED CITY
The walls of some buildings were all that was left standing in St Pierre. Rum
distilleries and warehouses exploded in the heat, adding to the destruction.
Many died in the cathedral, where mass for Ascension Day had just begun.

PROTECTING ANGEL?
This angel figurine, made of
corroded metal, is just recognisable.
Unlike Pompeii and Herculaneum,
no great works of art have been
uncovered in St Pierre.

Heap of glass melted
beyond recognition

Charred mug

Squashed candlestick

PETRIFIED
Wood, bone, ceramics, and most foods
contain carbon. Some of these organic
compounds were scorched or burned
completely. Others were carbonised
(pp.26–27), retaining enough of
their shape to be recognisable.

HOT ENOUGH TO MELT METAL
Some metal objects melted or partly
melted. This heap of iron nails was
fused together. The metal spoon lost
part of its bowl, where the metal
was thinnest. The candlestick was
squashed, probably when the building
it was in collapsed (it shows little sign
of melting). Copper telephone wires
in the town were not melted, so the
cloud must have been a little less than
1,083°C (1,981°F), the melting point
of copper.

*Carbonised
coffee beans*

Heap of fused
iron nails

ETERNAL FIGURE
The wooden cross
was burned right off
this crucifix, leaving
the figure of Jesus with
outstretched arms.

THE BARNUM & BAILEY
GREATEST SHOW ON EARTH

LUDGER SYLBARIS
THE ONLY LIVING OBJECT THAT SURVIVED IN THE "SILENT CITY OF DEATH" WHERE 40,000 HUMAN BEINGS
WERE SUFFOCATED, BURNED OR BURIED BY ONE BELCHING BLAST OF MONT PELEE'S TERRIBLE VOLCANIC ERUPTION

Melted metal spoon

Fused coins

OUT OF THE FRYING PAN
One of the two people left alive in St Pierre was Auguste
Ciparis. A prisoner condemned to death, he survived because
his cell had thick walls with one tiny window that faced away
from the volcano. He was later pardoned and went on to tour
the world as a circus act under the name of Ludger Sylbaris.

Affecting the world's weather

A BIG ASHY VOLCANIC ERUPTION has a dramatic effect on the weather. Dark days, severe winds, and heavy falls of rain or even mud may plague the local area for months. If the gas and dust are lofted high into the atmosphere, they may travel great distances around the globe. When this happens, the climate of the whole planet can be altered. The volcanic material filters out some sunlight, reducing temperatures down below. The high-flung particles also affect our views of the Sun and Moon by scattering sunlight of certain frequencies while allowing other wavelengths through. This can cause spectacular sunrises and sunsets. The Sun and Moon may seem to be wrapped in haloes or glow with strange colours. Two big eruptions in 1783 posed problems for later polar explorers, who encountered unusually thick pack ice. In the longer term, volcanic particles may cause global cooling, mass extinctions, or even ice ages.

EARLY EARTH
About 4,000 million years ago, planet Earth had no atmosphere and its surface was covered with erupting volcanoes. All the water in the oceans and many of the gases that make up the atmosphere have been produced by volcanoes erupting over the millennia.

LITTLE ICE AGE
Two major eruptions in 1783 – Skaftar in Iceland (p.24) and Asama in Japan – were followed by several very cold winters in Europe and America.

VOLCANIC SUNSETS
In 186 CE, the Chinese noted unusually red sunrises and sunsets. These were caused by volcanic emissions from the huge eruption of Mount Taupo in New Zealand. This sunset was caused by dust from the 1980 eruption of nearby Mount St Helens.

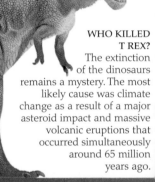

WHO KILLED T REX?
The extinction of the dinosaurs remains a mystery. The most likely cause was climate change as a result of a major asteroid impact and massive volcanic eruptions that occurred simultaneously around 65 million years ago.

FLOATING AROUND THE GLOBE
The June 1991 eruptions of Mount Pinatubo in the Philippines (right and p.17) spewed ash and gas into the stratosphere. Satellite images (above) showed that by 25 July the particles had spread around the world.

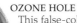

OZONE HOLE
This false-coloured satellite image shows the hole in the ozone layer over the Antarctic. The sulphur particles that Pinatubo threw high into the atmosphere may cause further damage to this protective layer. This could affect world temperatures.

80		18	12		
3				1	1
Vesuvius	Tambora	Krakatau	Katmai	St Helens	El Chichón
Italy	Indonesia	Indonesia	Alaska	USA	Mexico
79 CE	1815	1883	1912	1980	1982

COMPARING THE SIZE OF ERUPTIONS
The amount of ash a volcano emits is a good measure of the size of the eruption. This diagram compares total emissions of six major eruptions. The units are cubic km. Some large eruptions are relatively unknown. Mount Katmai covered remote parts of Alaska with huge quantities of ash in 1912, and the massive Tambora eruption of 1815 killed more than 90,000 Indonesians. Mount Pinatubo erupted 7 cubic km of ash in 1991.

An artist's impression of the 1883 eruption of Krakatau, Indonesia

ONCE IN A BLUE MOON
In 1883, the Indonesian island of Krakatau (or Krakatoa) was literally blown to pieces in a cataclysmic eruption (p.57). The explosion, one of the loudest ever recorded, was heard 4,000 km (2,400 miles) away at Alice Springs in Australia. Dust and gas coloured sunsets in Europe, where the Moon and the Sun even appeared to be blue or green. Floating islands of pumice drifted across the Indian Ocean for months afterwards, causing a great hazard to ships. This piece was washed up on a beach in Madagascar, 7,000 km (4,200 miles) away.

Steam vents and boiling mud

WHERE VOLCANIC HEAT WARMS an area, the water in the ground is heated too. During long dormant periods, the hot water may shoot to the surface in geysers, steam vents, hot springs, and pools of bubbling mud. These hydrothermal (hot water) features make for spectacular scenery in places as far apart as Japan, New Zealand, Iceland, Italy, and the USA. The hot water can also be harnessed to do useful work, providing it is not too acidic and its flow is constant. Steam can be directed to spin turbines and generate electricity. In Iceland, hot groundwater is piped into cities where it is used to heat homes and greenhouses. Many active volcanoes also release steam and other gases between eruptions, and changes in their gas emissions may give clues to future eruptions.

VULCAN, GOD OF FIRE
The ancient Romans believed Solfatara volcano near Naples, Italy, was an entrance to the underworld. It was also one of the workshops of the divine blacksmith, Vulcan – hence our word "volcano".

MEASURING THE EARTH'S HEAT
A thermocouple (p.43) is being used to measure the heat of a steam vent or fumarole in Solfatara crater. Temperatures here get up to 140°C (285°F). Changes in heat and gas emissions can give clues to future eruptions. They are also monitored before the geothermal energy of an area is tapped. Wild swings make the energy hard to harness.

WORKING UP A SWEAT
The fumaroles in Solfatara exude acid gases as well as steam. This observatory built in the 19th century is being eaten up by fumarole activity. Where the steam emerges in caverns or grottoes, it is believed to have miraculous healing powers. Since Roman times, visitors have been taking steam baths to treat arthritis and respiratory problems, or just to get the rumoured benefits of a good sweat.

CRYSTALS OF SULPHUR
The sulphur in volcanic gas cools and crystallises. In the right conditions, the yellow crystals of this non-metallic element grow large and translucent. These huge crystals are from Sicily, where sulphur has been mined for centuries. Sulphur has many uses, particularly in manufacturing. It is added to rubber to make it more durable in a process named after the Roman fire god – vulcanisation.

BUBBLING MUD

Some fumaroles bubble up through a mud bath of their own making. The acid sulphur gases corrode the rock they pass through, creating a great pool (or "pot") of soft mud. The bubbles burst at the surface with strange plopping sounds. The mud in this pot at Solfatara is 60°C (140°F). Some mud pots are much hotter, while others are cool enough for people to wallow in. These mud baths are popular beauty treatments that leave human skin feeling soft and silky.

SMELLY GAS

Spiky growths of sulphur crystals can be clearly seen around this fumarole vent. Close to the vent, the hot, smelly gases are invisible. Like the steam from a kettle spout, they only show up when the water vapour begins to condense a few centimetres away.

ROMAN BATHS

The ancient Romans liked the luxury of hot, running water and built huge public baths. Baths fed by natural hot springs became medical centres where sick people came to bathe in the mineral-rich water. Many of these spa towns still flourish, and invalids travel great distances to come and "take the waters".

Crust of tiny sulphur crystals from fumarole in Java, Indonesia

Souvenir plate showing Old Faithful Geyser, USA (p.7)

HOT WATER POWER

About 40 per cent of Iceland's electricity comes from hydrothermal power stations. As the technology improves, this figure is increasing, and other volcanically active countries like Japan, the USA, and New Zealand are developing their hydrothermal power programmes.

Sleeping beauties

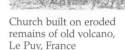

Church built on eroded remains of old volcano, Le Puy, France

VOLCANOES SOMETIMES SLEEP (lie dormant) for years or even centuries between eruptions. In this dormant period, volcanic gases may seep gently from the cooling magma that lies beneath the volcano. As these gases rise through the rocks of the volcano mountain, they react chemically with the minerals already in the rocks to create new minerals. These are often brightly coloured with large crystals. At the Earth's surface, the gases fume gently off into the atmosphere. The crater left at the end of the last eruption gradually weathers. Vegetation grows over the new rocks (pp.40–41), and erosion by wind and water makes slopes less steep. If the period of dormancy is tens of thousands of years, it may be difficult to recognise that a volcano ever existed. At that stage it may at last be safe to assume that the volcano is extinct.

Radiating zeolite crystals from the Faëroe Islands

BORN IN THE LAVA
Zeolite crystals grow in old gas bubbles in lava. They are found in a great variety of colours and forms.

Adventurers descend into the crater of Hekla, Iceland, in 1868.

AGATES
These beautiful banded stones form in cavities in cooled or cooling volcanic rocks. The bands, each one formed at a different time, are coloured by oxides and hydroxides of iron.

Outer layers of this agate are oldest

CRATER LAKE
Craters often fill with rainwater between eruptions. This crater lake, on the volcano Shirane in Japan, is very acidic, thanks to gas seeping up from the magma chamber below and dissolving in the water (pp.20–21). During an eruption, the acidic water may be hurled out of the crater. Mixed with hot rock and debris, it could race downhill in a deadly mud flow (pp.56–57).

Brightly coloured rocks seen at Solfatara (pp.36–37) by Lord Hamilton and illustrated by Pietro Fabris

Cut diamond

Olivine from St John's Island in the Red Sea

Forged in the fiery furnace

Hot volcanic fluids concentrate some unusual chemical elements. These cool slowly inside gas bubbles or other cavities in the volcanic rock. The slow crystallisation produces large, perfectly-formed crystals which can be cut and polished into gemstones. The harder stones are the most prized because they last forever. Diamond is the hardest stone of all, but softer stones are valued for their rich colours.

Uncut diamond in volcanic rock from the mantle, from Kimberley in South Africa

Cut peridot

RED SEA GEM
Gem-quality olivine is a deep green colour. The gem is known as peridot.

Agate-lined geode (cavity) from Brazil

BIRTH OF A CALDERA
During a large ashy eruption, the empty magma chamber may not be able to support the weight of the volcano's slopes. These collapse inwards, leaving a huge circular depression called a caldera. Calderas may be many kilometres across.

SANTORINI (THERA)
This island is the rim of a caldera formed by a huge volcanic eruption c. 1620 BCE. The massive explosion may have led to the collapse of the Minoan civilisation on the neighbouring island of Crete. These events may even be the basis of the myth of Atlantis, an island said to have been destroyed in a fiery apocalypse.

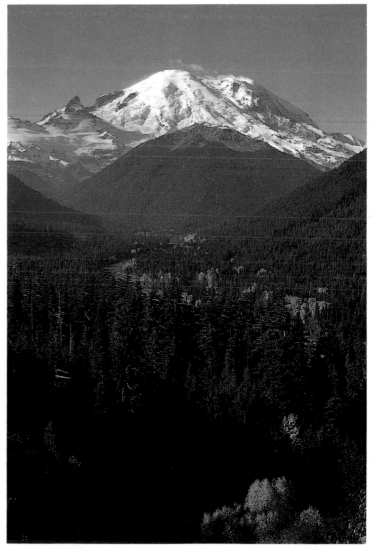

CASCADE VOLCANO
Mount Rainier is one of a chain of volcanoes in the Cascade Range that includes Mount St Helens (pp.14–15). Any of them could become active again one day. There are no written records, but Mount Rainier probably erupted several times in the 19th century. These events have been dated from tree rings, which show a stunting of growth following an eruption.

Life returns to the lava

A VOLCANIC ERUPTION has a profound effect on the landscape. All over the world, the land itself is a priceless resource where crops are grown to feed the population. For the landowner and farmer, an eruption that produces less than 20 cm (8 in) of ash is a blessing. The ash is full of nutrients which enrich the soil. But too much free fertilizer is catastrophic. The worst case for the farmer is when the land is overrun by lava flows. Thick flows can take months to cool. Decades (and in harsh climates even centuries) may pass while mosses and lichens spread slowly across the barren lavascape. Flowering plants and finally trees follow. The upper surface of the solid rock is slowly weathered, and the roots of the plants help to break it down to form soil. Only when a rich soil covers the land is it lush and fertile again. This process may take generations.

1944 lava flow, Mount Vesuvius

Raw lava

Dense, interlocking crystal structure

A few lichens find a home on the lava

PUTTING DOWN ROOTS
A fern takes root in a ropy pahoehoe lava flow less than a year old on the slopes of Kilauea volcano, Hawaii (pp.22–23).

Lichen covers the lava, providing a soft surface for other organisms

GATHERING MOSS
How quickly lava is recolonised by plants depends on the nature of the erupted material. Ashy pyroclastic material is recolonised the fastest. Plants are slowest in taking root on lava flows. The climate and altitude are also important – recolonisation is fastest in the Tropics. These pieces of lava are all from the same 1944 aa flow on the west slope of Mount Vesuvius in Italy. Some 47 years later, lichen covers a lot of the flow, and moss, grasses, and weedy flowering plants are taking root. The only trees, small pines, were planted by the government.

Grasses, often the first flowering plants

Beginnings of topsoil

Lichen cling to exposed parts of rock

Rock breaks down to soil, and grass and moss take root

Two species of moss grow in thin soil

New cone is still bare ash

Monte Somma, part of caldera left by huge, prehistoric eruption

Pine forests covers lower slopes

Mount Vesuvius steaming after mild eruption of 1855

BIRTH OF AN ISLAND
In November 1963, an undersea eruption off the southwest of Iceland gave birth to a new island, Surtsey (p.20). On the third day (above), eruptions were still highly explosive.

WASHED ASHORE
Seeds blown over or washed up on the beach of Surtsey soon took root in nearby ashfields (above). The beach itself was too harsh for most plants to live on.

THROUGH THE GRAPEVINE
The lush land around Vesuvius has been fertilised by ash from regular eruptions over the last 20 centuries. The ash supports a large grape harvest, which in turn supports the local wine industry.

LACRIMA CHRISTI
Mount Vesuvius is illustrated on the label of this wine grown on the volcano's slopes. Without the potassium, phosphorus, and other plant nutrients which the volcanic ash brings to the fields, the vines would not grow so thickly and the wine would taste less sweet.

Peacock butterfly lives on nectar of flowering plants

Weedy flowering plant

Eventually, soil cover is thick enough to support larger plants.

Lacrima Christi
DEL VESUVIO
DENOMINAZIONE DI ORIGINE CONTROLLATA
ITALIA
IMBOTTIGLIATO DA
Saviano
CASA VINICOLA · FONDATA NEL 1760
0.75 L ℮   18 ★ NA   12% vol.
OTTAVIANO
(NAPOLI · ITALIA)

FLOWER OF LYDIA
This brilliantly coloured shrub, a kind of broom, is one of the first plants to grow on the lava at Vesuvius.

ROMAN AMPHORAE
The stacks of amphorae for storing wine and olive oil found at Pompeii (pp.26–31) show how fertile the soil was in Roman times.

Mosaic from Pompeii of Venus, Roman goddess of fertility

Being a volcanologist

FOR A VOLCANOLOGIST – a scientist who watches, records, and interprets volcanoes – life can get uncomfortably hot. Volcanologists spend years monitoring volcanoes to try and predict when and how they will next erupt. Most of their time is spent analysing data in an office or laboratory, but fieldwork on the slopes of active or erupting volcanoes is vital. This involves taking lava and gas samples and measuring changes in temperature and landforms – sometimes while having to wear protective clothing. Hope of accurate predictions rose in the early 2000s, when scientists identified vibrations, or tremors, lasting a minute or more. They occur when magma forces its way upwards through cracks inside the volcano. As their frequency increases, scientists hope to be able to predict the time of an eruption.

KATIA KRAFFT
French volcanologists Katia and Maurice Krafft devoted their lives to documenting volcanoes. This photo taken by Maurice shows Katia observing a fire fountain in a protective suit. The husband and wife team were killed during the eruption of Mount Unzen in Japan in 1991.

SPACED-OUT SUIT
This protective suit has a metal coating which reflects the intense heat of a volcanic eruption and leaves the scientist inside cool. But it also inhibits the wearer from feeling, hearing, or seeing what is going on. In a tight spot, the bulky suit may stop him or her from running away to safety.

VOLCANO BIOGRAPHY
The volcanologist's notebook is the history of a volcano, rather like a chapter out of its biography. The observer makes notes and sketches of all the big (and little) events during an eruption. The significance of some things may only become clear later.

HOT ROD

This metal rod is ideal for collecting red-hot lava. From relative safety at one end of the pole, the volcanologist dips the far end into the lava flow. He or she then twists it around, hooking up a blob of lava. This cools quickly once it is pulled out of the main flow.

Hard hat

Binoculars

TAPE MEASURE

A tape measure is handy to check up on cracks in the ground which may widen imperceptibly from day to day.

Gloves made from the heat-resistant mineral asbestos

A CLOSER LOOK

Binoculars allow people to get closer to a volcano (in this case, Kilauea in Hawaii) without getting too close.

TOO HOT TO HANDLE

To collect warm samples and work close to red-hot lava, volcanologists wear asbestos gloves. Hard hats protect against small volcanic bombs (p.18).

Spirit level

PATHFINDER

The ground of an erupting volcano is continually changing, as new lava hardens into rock and builds new landforms. The mining transit is a surveying tool that is very good for simple, rapid mapping. It has a compass and a spirit level (to find verticals and horizontals). Small and light, it can be clipped onto the volcanologist's belt.

Compass

Rotating stage

Thermometer reading up to 250°C

MAPPING THE MOVING EARTH

A precise level can detect the small changes in ground level that foretell an eruption.

Folding, portable tripod

TAKING THE VOLCANO'S TEMPERATURE

Katia Krafft risks searing heat to take the temperature of a lava flow on Piton de la Fournaise volcano, Réunion (pp.22–23). She is not using a glass thermometer, which would melt, but a kind of electric thermometer called a thermocouple. The reading was 1,100°C (2,012°F), 300°C (540°F) less than the melting point of steel.

Volcanoes on other planets

SPACE EXPLORATION HAS SHOWN that volcanic activity is one of the most important geological processes in the Solar System. The many space missions of the last two decades have brought back photographs and even rock samples. Some craft will never return to Earth, but continue to travel into deep space, beaming back information that can be translated by computers into detailed images of the more distant planets. We now know that many planetary bodies are scarred by enormous craters. But few of these are volcanic. Most are impact craters, the scars left by collisions with meteorites. Like Earth, the Moon, Venus, and Mars have solid surfaces that have been partly shaped by volcanic activity. The volcanoes on the Moon and Mars have been extinct for many millions of years. Scientists suspect that Venus's volcanoes may still be active. But of all the other planets in our solar system, only Io, one of Jupiter's 16 moons, shows volcanoes that are still active and erupting.

TIDYING THE PLANET
The hero of Antoine de Saint-Exupéry's children's story *The Little Prince* lives on a planet (Asteroid B–612) with two active volcanoes. Before setting out on a journey, he cleans them out to be sure they won't erupt and make trouble while he's away; he knows this could happen if their throats get blocked and they cannot breathe. He also cleans out his one extinct volcano, because, as he says, "One never knows!"

molten rock

lava flow

SURFACE OF IO
This coloured infrared image shows the Tvashtar Catena volcanic region on the surface of Io, one of Jupiter's moons. The image was taken by NASA's *Galileo Orbiter* spacecraft and shows molten rock and a 60-km- (37-mile-) long lava flow, produced by a volcanic eruption.

OLYMPUS MONS
The extinct volcano Olympus Mons is 600 km (370 miles) across and rises 25 km (15 miles) above the surrounding plain. This makes it the highest point on planet Mars – and the largest volcano yet found in the universe, bigger than the entire Hawaiian island chain (pp. 22–23). Huge calderas (p.39) nest one inside each other at its summit.

Clouds of ice shroud the summit

Volcano Sif

Volcano Gula

ERUPTING INTO SPACE
One of the most exciting discoveries in the exploration of the Solar System was the erupting volcano Prometheus on Io. Seen in this *Voyager* image, the volcano is spewing a plume of gases 160 km (100 miles) above the solid surface. The plume looks pale against the black of space. The eruption clouds shoot far into space because Io has very low gravity and virtually no atmosphere.

BENEATH THE CLOUDS
The spacecraft *Magellan* used imaging radar to penetrate the dense atmosphere of Venus. The images revealed huge volcanoes and impact craters lurking beneath the clouds. Like most features on Venus, they were named after women, including goddesses from mythology.

Vidicon camera viewer

SPACE VOYAGERS

The two *Voyagers* were launched in 1977. They flew past Jupiter in 1979 and Saturn in 1980–1981. This is a model of *Voyager One*, which went as far as Saturn before heading off into space. *Voyager Two* flew by Uranus in 1986. In 1989, 12 years after its launch, it sent back data from Neptune.

Lava flows

300-km-(190-mile-) high gas plume from volcano Pele

SHOOTING THE STARS

The two *Voyager* craft caught eight of Io's volcanoes in the act of erupting. They also saw about 200 huge calderas, some filled with what seem to be active lava lakes. The images were collected by Vidicon, a type of TV camera that uses an electron gun and a photoconductor. The information is collected digitally and transmitted back to Earth as a series of picture elements (pixels) arranged in lines. These are then processed and coloured to create simulated "photos".

Dark, inactive volcano, Babbar Patera

Propulsion fuel tank for making delicate adjustments to flight path

When the earth moves

BEING IN A LARGE EARTHQUAKE is a terrifying experience. The shaking of the ground we stand on is profoundly disturbing, both physically and psychologically. When the shaking starts there is no knowing how long it will go on or how severe it will be. Only when it stops is there some certainty in life again. The longest tremor ever recorded, the Alaskan earthquake of 23 March, 1964, lasted four minutes (p.57). But most quakes last less than a minute. In those brief moments, homes, shops, even entire cities are destroyed. The earth sometimes seems to undulate. Afterwards, great cracks may appear in the ground. Even stranger, the rocks may show no sign at all of the intense undulations they went through in the shaking. People also seem to find the many months of small earthquakes (aftershocks) which follow a big tremor very disturbing.

Cartoon about the San Francisco quake of 1906, captioned "I hope I never have one of those splitting headaches again."

DISASTER MOVIE
This film about an earthquake destroying Los Angeles was shown in "Sensurround" – low frequency sounds meant to simulate earthquake shaking.

SHAKEN TO THE FOUNDATIONS
Almost 75 years old, these wood buildings in the Marina district of San Francisco had been built on a land-fill site. They slipped off their foundations as the filled land settled in the shaking of the 1989 earthquake (p.7).

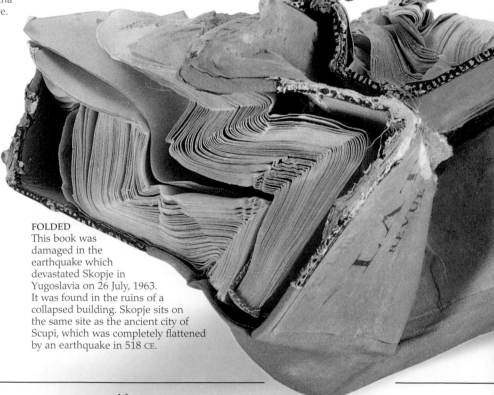

FOLDED
This book was damaged in the earthquake which devastated Skopje in Yugoslavia on 26 July, 1963. It was found in the ruins of a collapsed building. Skopje sits on the same site as the ancient city of Scupi, which was completely flattened by an earthquake in 518 CE.

PANIC SETS IN
People leave buildings and rush into the streets in panic as an earthquake shakes the city of Valparaiso, Chile in 1906. Masonry buildings are collapsing as their walls crumble.

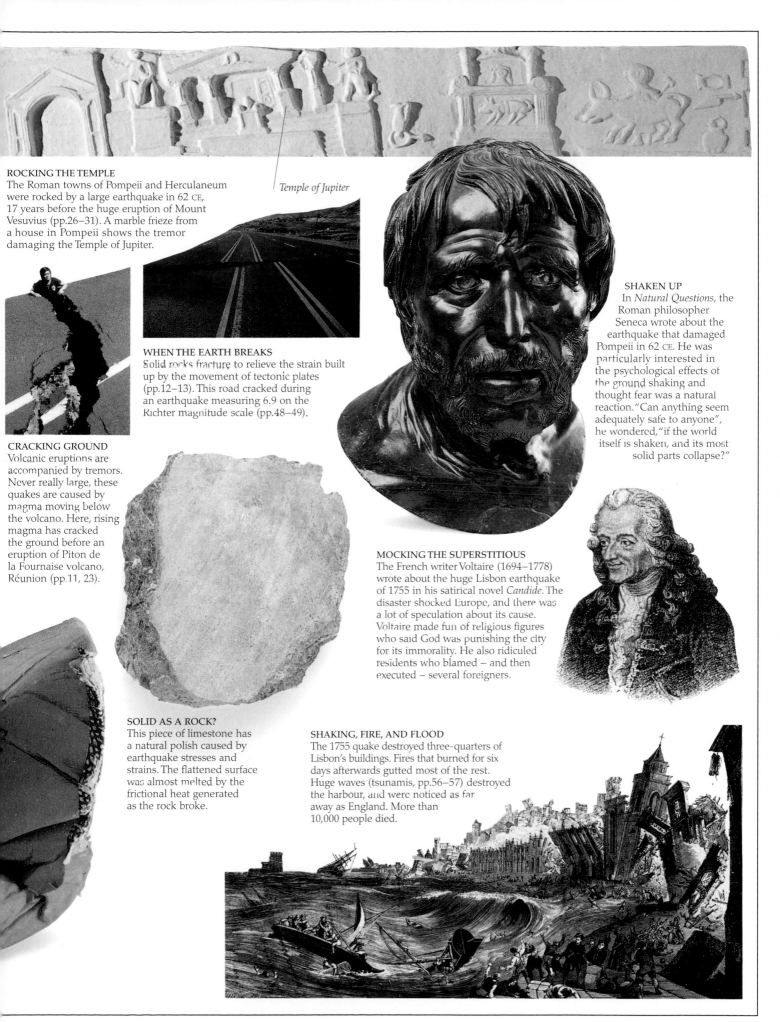

ROCKING THE TEMPLE
The Roman towns of Pompeii and Herculaneum were rocked by a large earthquake in 62 CE, 17 years before the huge eruption of Mount Vesuvius (pp.26–31). A marble frieze from a house in Pompeii shows the tremor damaging the Temple of Jupiter.

Temple of Jupiter

WHEN THE EARTH BREAKS
Solid rocks fracture to relieve the strain built up by the movement of tectonic plates (pp.12–13). This road cracked during an earthquake measuring 6.9 on the Richter magnitude scale (pp.48–49).

CRACKING GROUND
Volcanic eruptions are accompanied by tremors. Never really large, these quakes are caused by magma moving below the volcano. Here, rising magma has cracked the ground before an eruption of Piton de la Fournaise volcano, Réunion (pp.11, 23).

SHAKEN UP
In *Natural Questions*, the Roman philosopher Seneca wrote about the earthquake that damaged Pompeii in 62 CE. He was particularly interested in the psychological effects of the ground shaking and thought fear was a natural reaction. "Can anything seem adequately safe to anyone", he wondered, "if the world itself is shaken, and its most solid parts collapse?"

MOCKING THE SUPERSTITIOUS
The French writer Voltaire (1694–1778) wrote about the huge Lisbon earthquake of 1755 in his satirical novel *Candide*. The disaster shocked Europe, and there was a lot of speculation about its cause. Voltaire made fun of religious figures who said God was punishing the city for its immorality. He also ridiculed residents who blamed – and then executed – several foreigners.

SOLID AS A ROCK?
This piece of limestone has a natural polish caused by earthquake stresses and strains. The flattened surface was almost melted by the frictional heat generated as the rock broke.

SHAKING, FIRE, AND FLOOD
The 1755 quake destroyed three-quarters of Lisbon's buildings. Fires that burned for six days afterwards gutted most of the rest. Huge waves (tsunamis, pp.56–57) destroyed the harbour, and were noticed as far away as England. More than 10,000 people died.

Intensity and magnitude

How do you measure the size of an earthquake? News reports usually give the quake a magnitude on the Richter scale. The Richter magnitude is useful because it can be worked out from a recording – called a seismogram – of the earthquake waves (pp.52–55). The waves of a big quake can be recorded on the other side of the globe. So as long as the distance between the recording device and the quake's centre is taken into account, the Richter magnitude can be calculated from anywhere on the planet. But where the shaking is felt, it is more important to know how intense the shaking was and how it affected buildings and people. This is called the intensity of shaking. It is measured on a different scale such as the Modified Mercalli Intensity Scale. Intensity is purely descriptive and cannot be recorded by a machine. Instead it is compiled by inspecting the damage and getting the quake's survivors to fill in questionnaires. Every earthquake has just one Richter magnitude. But because the damage it does falls off away from its centre, it has many intensities, which also fall off away from the centre.

Giuseppe Mercalli (1850–1914)

Intensity

The Italian volcanologist Giuseppe Mercalli created his intensity scale in 1902. He used 12 grades with Roman numerals from I to XII. His scale was later updated to create the Modified Mercalli Intensity Scale.

I The shaking is not felt by people, but instruments record it.

II People at rest notice the shaking (above), especially if they are on the upper floors of buildings. Delicately suspended objects may swing.

III People indoors feel a vibration like the passing of a light truck. Hanging objects swing (above). Length of shaking can be estimated, but people may not recognise it as an earthquake.

IV Vibration like a heavy truck passing. Dishes rattle and wooden walls creak. Standing cars rock.

V Felt outdoors. Liquid in glasses slops out (above), small objects knocked over. Doors swing open and close.

VI Felt by all. Many are frightened and rush outdoors. People walk unsteadily; windows, dishes break (above). Pictures fall off walls; small bells ring.

Magnitude

Working in California in the 1930s, Charles Richter wanted to compare the sizes of local earthquakes. He used the wiggly tracings of the shaking which are recorded on seismographs (pp.52–55). Knowing how far he was from each quake, he applied a distance factor to the maximum wiggle. After allowing for the characteristics of the instrument, he came up with the quake's magnitude. Richter's scale is used today all over the world.

American seismologist
Charles F. Richter
(1900–1985)

RECORDING THE SHAKES
Richter took the smallest earthquake he could record at the time and called it magnitude zero. Today's instruments are much more sensitive, so the smallest quakes they register are given negative magnitudes. The highest Richter magnitudes recorded are about 9.

Intensity contours for an earthquake that struck Japan on 22 May, 1925

Epicentre

II III IV V VI

VII Difficult to stand (above). Furniture broken, plaster and loose bricks crack and fall. Waves on ponds. Large bells ring.

VIII Steering of cars affected. Damage to masonry walls, some of which fall. Falling chimneys, steeples (above), monuments. Branches off trees. Changes in flow of wells and springs. Cracks in wet ground.

IX General panic. Animals run to and fro in confusion. General damage to foundations of buildings. Frame buildings, if not bolted down, shifted off their foundations (above). Sand, mud, and water bubble out of ground.

X Most masonry and frame buildings destroyed with their foundations (above). Some well-built wooden buildings destroyed. Large landslides. Water thrown out of rivers and canals.

XI Railway lines greatly distorted. Underground pipelines completely out of service. Highways useless. Ground distorted by large cracks. Many large landslips and rock falls.

XII Practically all built structures above and below ground destroyed or useless (above). Ground surface much altered with cracks and slumps. River courses moved, waterfalls appear. Waves seen on ground surface.

Waves of destruction

Earthquake waves travel fast – about 25,000 kph (16,000 mph) in rock, rather slower in soft sands and muds. In the seconds after the rock fracture that causes earthquake shaking, shock waves travel out in all directions. Usually they are most devastating near the epicentre, the spot on the surface nearest to where the rocks have fractured. But sometimes the waves are slowed down and concentrated by soft sands and muds. This can cause severe shaking even far from the epicentre. The first waves to arrive are primary or P waves. They are fastest because they travel like sound waves, with a push-pull movement that does not distort the rock they pass through very much. The slower secondary or S waves are the next to arrive. They travel at slightly more than half the speed, as they distort the rocks in a more complicated sideways-shearing movement. The slowest waves, surface waves, move in the most complex way. They only develop properly a long way from the epicentre.

SEISMOGRAM

This is a recording of a 5.1 Richter magnitude quake. The time lag between the P and S waves - in this case, 17 seconds - is used to calculate the distance from the focus. The magnitude is calculated from the maximum P-wave amplitude, taking into account the distance and the sensitivity of the seismograph.

P wave of maximum amplitude

Time scale

— 17 seconds —

First P wave   First S wave

LOCATING AN EARTHQUAKE

Eskdalemuir, Scotland

Epicentre in Caspian Sea

Hyderabad, India

Lusaka, Zambia

On 17 September, 1989, seismologists in Scotland recorded a quake of magnitude 6.1. They calculated how far away it had occurred and drew a circle across the globe with this distance as its radius. Two other stations - in Africa and India - made calculations and drew distance circles. They met in the Caspian Sea, the epicentre of the quake.

Epicentre   *Focus*

DEEP FOCUS

An earthquake's focus - the area where the rocks have fractured - is usually many kilometres inside the Earth. On the surface, the waves are strongest at the epicentre, the point directly above the focus.

Seismic station records first P-waves

Church bells ring

People hear low rumbling like thunder

Animals are restless, and may rush about and cry

Startled by ripples, water birds fly off ponds

P waves

BEFORE THE EARTHQUAKE

Animals (and some people) may feel uncomfortable in the minutes before an earthquake strikes. They seem to sense that something is not quite right.

THE FIRST WAVES STRIKE

The first waves to arrive, P waves, may be so small that they are heard but not felt.

DEVASTATED IN A MINUTE
The town of Pointe-à-Pitre on the Caribbean island of Guadeloupe was shaken by an earthquake of Richter magnitude 8 on 8 February, 1843. Eyewitnesses said the shaking lasted for about a minute. This was long enough to reduce most of the buildings to ruins. A fire that followed torched what was left of the town.

Woman sits by the ruins of her house in Lice, Turkey

Living through an earthquake

This model shows the waves of shaking from a large earthquake as they pass through the countryside. The epicentre is far off the page to the right. The fast P waves (in yellow) have gone the farthest and are about to strike the area on the far left. S waves (blue) follow, causing considerable damage. The slowest waves, surface waves (red), arrive seconds later. They have just reached the right of the model, where they have caused the total collapse of buildings already weakened by the S waves.

Trees and bushes shake and rustle

Ground cracks open

Cracks appear in buildings

Vehicles cannot follow straight lines

Sand and water bubble out of ground for hours after shaking stops

Fires start in ruins

Trees are uprooted

Landslide

People panic, have trouble standing up

Many buildings in ruins

S waves

Surface waves

SECONDARY WAVES STRIKE
The S waves follow the P waves. Here the waves are shaking and distorting buildings until they crack or even collapse.

SURFACE WAVES
Some quakes generate powerful surface waves. They can cause serious damage far from the epicentre.

Measuring earthquake waves

THE FIRST INSTRUMENT FOR RECORDING EARTHQUAKES was built by the Chinese scientist Zhang Heng in the second century CE. The original instrument did not survive and we only know of it from contemporary descriptions. It was a huge device about 2 m (6 ft) across and built of bronze. It could record earthquakes too slight to be noticed otherwise. The device could also tell roughly which direction the quake had come from. But because it gave no more information, we now call it a seismoscope. Not until 1856, soon after the discovery of electricity, was a more sophisticated earthquake recorder invented. Built by the Italian Luigi Palmieri, it is a seismograph, a device that writes a permanent trace – known as a seismogram – of the earthquake shaking. It was also set up to measure the overall size of the earthquake shaking (pp.48–49).

EARLY SEISMOLOGIST
The Chinese were keeping lists of earthquakes as early as 780 BCE. In the fourth century BCE, the Greek philosopher Aristotle suggested that tremors were caused by unstable vapours. But it was not until 132 CE that the Chinese geographer and astronomer Zhang Heng (78–139) invented the first seismoscope.

Inner workings of Zhang Heng's seismoscope

Pendulum

Suspension mechanism pulls on dragon's mouth

TOADS AND DRAGONS
Zhang Heng's seismoscope is a bronze vessel ringed with dragons and toads. A heavy pendulum hangs inside. During a tremor, the vessel moves more than the heavy pendulum. This triggers one or more dragons to open their jaws. Bronze balls held there are released, dropping into the open mouths of the toads which wait below.

Ball held in dragon's mouth

The toad that is farthest from the epicentre catches the falling ball. This indicates which direction the quake came from

RING MY BELL
This is a reconstruction of a seismoscope built by the Italian naturalist and clockmaker Ascanio Filomarino in 1795. When the ground shook, the pendulum stayed still. But the rest of the apparatus shook, making bells ring and a clock tick. Filomarino was killed on the slopes of Mount Vesuvius by an angry mob who thought his experiments were ungodly. They also burned his work-shop and destroyed the seismoscope.

Clock starts ticking when shaking begins. if it is found at 3.00, the quake began three hours earlier

Clock stops when shaking starts

Ticker tape

Heavy weight of pendulum

Bells ring when quake starts

Pencil leaves trace on paper

Recording apparatus of Palmieri's seismograph, which produces a ticker tape record of the shaking

Four mercury-filled U-tubes make contact with platinum wires held just above the liquid metal

Ivory pulleys which only move in one direction record the maximum size of the oscillations

Wire of pendulum which records direction of tremor

Helical spring bounces in vertical movement of earthquake

PALMIERI'S SEISMOGRAPH
Luigi Palmieri (1807–1896) built the first seismograph. This, his original apparatus, has been recording quakes since 1856. It has two parts. The larger part (right), which contains tubes of mercury, detects earthquakes. The second part (top right) prints a record of them. With this device Palmieri discovered that small foreshocks sometimes precede large quakes and that tremors accompany volcanic eruptions.

Electrical circuit is completed when platinum point dips in the dish of mercury below

LUIGI PALMIERI
While observing the 1855 eruption of Vesuvius, Palmieri realised that an instrument that measured small ground tremors might help in predicting eruptions. This electromagnetic instrument was the result of his experiments with electricity.

VESUVIUS OBSERVATORY
Palmieri developed his device while he was director of this observatory near the crater of the active volcano.

Weight of pendulum

Maximum wave size recorded here

Continued on next page

TOKYO, 1923
The city of Tokyo after the huge quake of 1923. Houses built of wood and paper were set alight by overturned stoves. At least 200,000 died in the fire storm which followed (p.57).

Seismogram of 1923 Tokyo earthquake, recorded by Gray-Milne seismograph in Oxford, England

JOHN MILNE
An English geologist, John Milne (1850-1913) invented his own seismograph while he was teaching geology in Tokyo. He later set up the Seismological Society of Japan.

Seismometers

Instruments that capture earthquake motion are called seismometers. They include a recording device, the seismograph, and produce a record, the seismogram. All seismometers work on the principle, developed by Zhang Heng, that an earthquake shakes a heavy pendulum less than the surrounding ground.

Side view of Gray-Milne seismograph

Three pens write traces of vertical and two components of horizontal shaking

One of two pendulums which register horizontal shaking

SHAKING AROUND THE CLOCK
This seismograph, designed in 1885 by the Englishmen Thomas Gray and John Milne, was the first meant for non-stop use. It had three pendulums and three pens, to record the three components of ground motion – vertical, east-west horizontal, and north-south horizontal.

Clock to indicate the moment quake starts

54

A MODERN OBSERVATORY

At the Vesuvius Observatory, great reels of paper record the ground movement measured by a series of seismometers set up at strategic points in the area. Many modern earthquake stations place their seismometers in remote places or deep in boreholes. Here they are far from confusing signals like heavy car or air traffic or quarrying. Their data is beamed into the recording centre by radio or along telephone lines. Modern seismographs record on magnetic tape, which allows for much better analysis.

PORTABLE

Networks of portable seismometers are used to monitor aftershocks of big quakes and ground tremors during volcanic eruptions. They were also used to prove that earthquakes did not cause the Lake Nyos disaster (p.20).

MOONQUAKES

American astronauts left seismometers on the Moon to record moonquakes. Many moonquakes are caused by meteorites hitting the surface. Others seem to take place most often when the Moon is nearest to the Earth.

Case hides inverted, suspended pendulum

Paper drum winds very slowly between earthquakes. When shaking starts, gears change and the drum starts feeding the paper through much faster

Handle for winding up weight which turns drum

Damping system, which makes sure that each shock wave is only recorded once

Suspended weight drives paper drum (mechanical clocks driven in same way)

Smoked paper seismogram

Arm from which pendulums are suspended

SMOKING UP

Early seismographs, many still in use, scratch their traces on smoked paper. This avoids the problems of ink, which can run out or gum up – a disaster during tremors. The paper is smoked by coating it in the carbon produced by burning oil.

HEAVY DUTY

This is a restored version of the seismograph invented by the German Emil Wiechert (1861–1928) in 1908. Its 200 kg (440 lb) mass measures the two horizontal components of ground shaking. It worked in tandem with a smaller instrument that measured vertical motion. Here, an inverted pendulum consists of a stiff rod balanced on a movable base that is very sensitive to any horizontal motion. An even bigger Wiechert instrument has been operating at Uppsala in Sweden since 1904.

Mud, flood, and avalanche

THE TRAUMA OF AN EARTHQUAKE or volcanic eruption may have devastating repercussions. Large ash eruptions are often followed by landslides or mud flows. The ash that piles up near the crater may collapse, bringing part of the mountain down with it. Heavy rain often adds to the problem, creating a wet slurry that turns into a mud flow. In mountains, both quakes and eruptions may trigger avalanches; by or beneath the sea, they can both cause giant water waves. These are popularly known as "tidal waves". But as they are not created by tides, scientists prefer the Japanese name, *tsunami*. Tsunamis may travel across oceans. When they break on faraway shores, the great walls of water can wreak horrendous damage.

Overview of Armero mud flow, 1985

SWEPT AWAY
The ashy eruptions of Mount Pinatubo in the Philippines (p.17) were accompanied by mud flows which swept away roads, bridges, and several villages. The flows were caused by torrential rain falling on newly erupted ash.

BURIED IN A SEA OF MUD
In November 1985, an eruption of Ruiz volcano in Colombia, South America spewed clouds of ash and pumice onto the snow and ice fields of the mountain's summit. This melted part of the snow, which in turn wet the ash, turning it into a moving slurry. The heavy mud flow cascaded down the Lagunillas Canyon at speeds of up to 35 kph (20 mph). The city of Armero, 60 km (36 miles) away at the mouth of the canyon, was devastated by the roaring torrent of mud (left and below). Some 22,000 people were buried alive by the waves of mud, rock, and debris which set around them like wet concrete. The only survivors were rescued from the edge of the flow (p.58).

Lorry trapped in mud, Armero

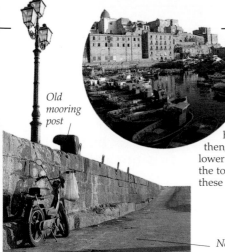

ABANDONED TOWN

Pozzuoli near Naples, Italy has been shaken by many small earthquakes. Part of the town was abandoned after shaking damage in 1983. The town has risen several metres since then, so the harbour had to be rebuilt lower down. Magma moving below the town is probably the cause of all these disturbances.

Old mooring post

New dock level

DWARFING FUJI

Japanese coastlines are plagued by tsunamis from both volcanic eruptions and earthquakes. The volcano Fujiyama (p.6) can be seen in the background of *Giant Wave*, a picture of a tsunami by Katsushika Hokusai (1760–1849).

TSUNAMI

In December 2004, movement along a submarine fault deep below the seabed of the eastern Indian Ocean generated a series of catastrophic tsunamis that spread out across the Indian Ocean. Coastal communities as far away as Sri Lanka and Africa suffered death and destruction but the highest death tolls were experienced in the islands of southeast Asia – in the village of Calang on Sumatra only 1,000 of a population of 5,000 survived.

KRAKATAU, WEST OF JAVA

Tsunamis as high as 30 m (100 ft) crashed into surrounding islands after the cataclysmic eruption of Krakatoa (now called Krakatau, p.35). The walls of water flattened many villages on Sumatra and Java (which is actually east of Krakatau), killing 36,000 people.

AVALANCHE

Earthquake shaking may trigger avalanches that were just waiting to happen. In 1970, a magnitude 7.7 quake off the coast of Peru caused a disastrous slide of snow and rock which fell 4,000 m (13,200 ft) and killed over 50,000 people in the valley below.

FIRE IN THE RUINS

Firefighters douse a blaze after the 1989 San Francisco earthquake (p.7). The fires that follow quakes or eruptions can raze cities to the ground. If gas mains are broken or inflammable liquids spilt, the slightest spark causes fire. Shaking often damages the underground water supply, making a blaze harder to fight. The large 1923 Tokyo quake (p.54) was followed by a terrifying fire storm that swept through the city's wooden houses and left 200,000 dead.

State of emergency

THE CHAOS THAT FOLLOWS a big earthquake or volcanic eruption makes rescue difficult and dangerous. Many people may be killed by collapsing buildings in the few seconds that violent earthquake shaking lasts. More die from injuries in the next few hours. But people trapped in fallen masonry may survive for days. For rescuers, finding them and getting them out is a race against time. It may be hard to rescue trapped people without putting more people at risk. Half-collapsed buildings may topple further at any moment. Hazardous substances could suddenly catch fire or explode. In ash-flow or mud-flow eruptions, no one knows when to expect another surge or flow. Damage to telephone lines, television and radio links, and electricity, gas, and water supplies makes rescue operations even harder to mount.

PERILOUS RESCUE
A survivor is lifted by helicopter from the setting mud in Armero, Colombia in 1985 (p.56).

MUDDY ESCAPE
An unconscious survivor is rescued from the mud flows that engulfed Armero in 1985. Some 60 km (36 miles) from the volcano, parts of the mud flow were still hot, and survivors had to be treated for burns.

Controls showing level of infra-red radiation

FINDING LIVE BODIES
A thermal image camera is used to locate people trapped after an earthquake. Survivors are often buried, wounded or unconscious, in the rubble of their collapsed homes. The camera uses infra-red radiation to detect the heat of a living person. The problem is distinguishing the heat of a body from the natural heat of other objects. This is easiest early in the morning, when the background heat is lowest.

Strap worn around neck ensures expensive camera is not dropped in rubble

HAVE CAMERA, WILL TRAVEL
The London Fire and Civil Defence Authority uses thermal image cameras to find survivors after all kinds of disasters. It sends trained teams to disaster zones, like northwest Iran after the massive quake of June 1990.

Searcher wears headphones to listen for human sounds in the wreckage

Italian newspaper illustration from 1906 showing a boy being rescued from the remains of his home after an earthquake

TRAPPED PERSON DETECTOR

This device was used after the Armenian earthquake of 1988. Thousands of people were buried when multi-storey buildings collapsed in heaps of rubble. Some were successfully located with this detector, which works by detecting vibrations.

Microphone, so rescuer can talk to trapped person

Red two-way electrode allows rescuer to converse with survivor

Yellow one-way electrode picks up vibrations

KASHMIR EARTHQUAKE

Some 38,000 people were killed in Pakistan in October 2005, when a magnitude 7.6 earthquake hit Kashmir. Many hill villages such as Balakot were almost completely destroyed.

SENSITIVE NOSE

Alongside technological equipment, sniffer dogs play their part in the race to find survivors after an earthquake. The aftershocks that usually follow the main quake are a big hazard. Rescuers are often at risk as they work in the precarious remains of buildings. If an aftershock causes further collapse, the rescuers may have to be rescued, too.

Italian magazines produced for the 1990s, the International Decade for Natural Disaster Reduction

Preparing for disaster

EARTHQUAKES AND VOLCANIC ERUPTIONS are natural events that have been happening throughout the Earth's history. As the planet's population increases, more and more people are living in danger zones, along faults or close to active volcanoes. When one of these natural events upsets human life, many people may die and their buildings and farmland may be destroyed. In the aftermath, disease and famine may be even more destructive. We cannot hope to stop disasters entirely. But as knowledge of the Earth's workings increases, wise planning can reduce their number and scale. Learning to live in disaster zones means actively monitoring volcanoes and fault lines and building cities that can withstand earthquake shaking. It also means education, so people know what to do in an emergency.

BUILDING CITIES THAT WON'T FALL DOWN
Many modern cities are in earthquake-prone regions. One way to reduce disaster is to design buildings that can withstand the deadly shaking. The Transamerica Pyramid looks precarious, but it is designed to be twice as strong as building codes for the San Francisco Bay area require. In a major quake, the structures at the base will reduce sway by a third.

LIVING IN THE SHADOW
Two thousand years after the volcano's greatest eruption, over two million people now live in the Bay of Naples in the shadow of Mount Vesuvius. This is modern Herculaneum, a thriving town that surrounds the ruins of Roman Herculaneum.

FRANK LLOYD WRIGHT
This American architect was a pioneer in the design of earthquake-resistant buildings. His Imperial Hotel in Tokyo survived the 1923 quake almost unscathed.

SHAKE TILL THEY DROP
Built in 1923, this pioneering Japanese shaking table was used to test models of buildings to see how they stood up to severe shaking. Modern shake tables are controlled by computers.

MOST MEASURED PLACE

The town of Parkfield in central California straddles the San Andreas fault system. Seismologists have predicted a major earthquake here. A laser measuring system is being used to detect movements along the fault. The laser, mounted on a hilltop in Parkfield, bounces light off a network of detectors several kilometres away on the other side of the fault. It can detect ground movement of less than a millimetre over six kilometres.

MEASURING CREEP

A technician for the US Geological Survey emerges from a creepmeter. He has been measuring creep, slow movement along the fault. Creep releases stress along the fault without detectable shaking.

LEARNING FROM PAST DISASTERS

Earthquakes of the same size tend to happen in the same place at regular intervals. Studying large quakes – in this case, the one that rocked Pompeii in 62 CE (p.47) – may help scientists to predict the next big tremor.

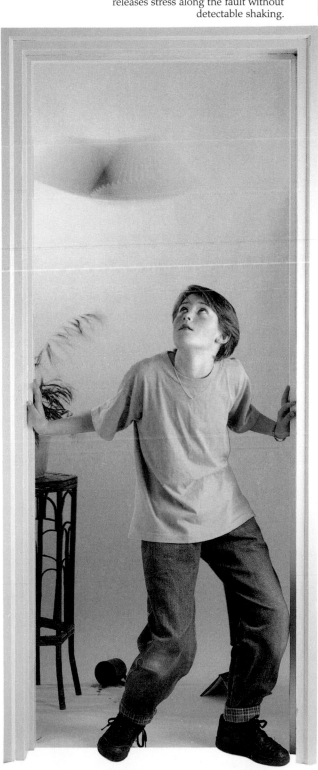

FALLING MASONRY

In this earthquake drill, rescue workers are treating actors "hit" by falling masonry. Many were injured by falling brick and stone in the 1989 San Francisco earthquake. Designing buildings without heavy architectural ornaments or chimneys might cut down on casualties like these.

Earthquake rescue practice in Japan

EARTHQUAKE DRILL

In Japan and California, earthquake drills are a part of everyday life. Children learn to keep a torch and good shoes by their beds, so they can get to safety even if a quake strikes at night. Many people rush outdoors, only to be hit by falling chimneys, roof tiles, or glass. The safest place indoors is under a solid piece of furniture like a table or beneath the frame of an archway or doorway.

Anger of the gods

As long as people have lived on Earth, they have been curious about natural events like earthquakes and volcanic eruptions. Myths are a way of recording or explaining these strange, often fantastic happenings. In many parts of the world, myths and legends handed down from generation to generation are the only history. Often these myths are not written down or have been put on the page only recently. Through the poetic language and spiritual ideas, it is sometimes possible to recognise real places or happenings. Most societies explain natural events as the workings of a god or gods. In this way they give the planet the kinds of emotions we expect from human beings. When the gods are angry, they may punish the people with the fire of an eruption or the horrible shaking of an earthquake. People often react to such disasters by offering sacrifices or gifts to calm the gods. Societies near active volcanoes may see the fiery mountains as the workshops of the gods (p.36). Many gods are believed to live on the eerie summits of volcanoes, which are often shrouded in fire and cloud.

Christians in Naples, Italy try to stop the 1906 eruption of Mount Vesuvius (p.31) with crosses and prayers

HUMAN SACRIFICE
In Nicaragua, the people once threw their most beautiful young women into the lava lake at Masaya to stop the volcano from erupting.

Lava lake

POPOCATEPETL
This Aztec illustration shows Popocatépetl, Mexico, one of the highest peaks in the Americas at 5,452 m (17,887 ft). Its name is Aztec for "smoking mountain". When the volcano erupted violently in the 1520s, the Aztecs believed the gods were angry at the Spanish *conquistadores* (conquerors) who had looted their temples.

RESPONSIBLE FROG
Many cultures believed that the ground they stood on was held up by some huge creature. The ancient Greeks and Romans thought the superhuman Atlas was carrying the weight (p.10). Mongolians believed in a gigantic frog. Each time the animal stumbled under his great burden, the ground shook with an earthquake. A similar Hindu myth says the Earth sits on the backs of eight giant elephants.

ONE-EYED GIANT
This is an aerial view of Mount Vesuvius. From above, such craters resemble giant eyes. They may have inspired the Greek myth of the Cyclops, a tribe of one-eyed giants who helped the fire god Hephaistos in his forge (below and p.36). Like craters, the Cyclops hurled fire and rocks when they were angry.

SHAKING THE SEA FLOOR
When the Greek sea god Poseidon (known as Neptune to the Romans) was angry, he banged the sea floor with his trident. This created earthquakes and tsunamis (pp.56-57).

Destruction of Sodom and Gomorrah, by an unknown Flemish painter

SODOM AND GOMORRAH
According to the Bible, God destroyed these cities with flood and fire because he was angry at their evil inhabitants. They may really have been devastated by some natural geological disaster.

Bronze figure of Hephaistos, first or second century BCE.

MASTER OF FIRE
The ancient Greeks believed the god Hephaistos had his fiery workshops under volcanoes (p.36). Another god, Prometheus, stole some of the fire from the volcanoes and gave it to the mortals – a way of explaining how people discovered fire.

WHEN THE GODS ARE AWAY...
A Japanese myth says earthquakes are caused by the writhings of a giant catfish. Normally the gods keep the rascal under control by pinning it down with a large rock. But during October, when the gods are away, the fish may get loose. This wood-block print shows the gods flying back over the ruins of Edo (now Tokyo) after a big quake in October 1855. The leader of the gods is carrying the rock.

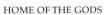

HOME OF THE GODS
Mount Fuji is thought to be the home of the god Kunitokotache (p.6). Fujiyama, the sacred spirit of the mountain, is said to protect the Japanese people. Legend says that the mountain can only be climbed by the pure of spirit. Many thousands make the ascent to the summit each year.

Did you know?

FASCINATING FACTS

Much of New Zealand's North Island, some 20,000 sq km (7,722 sq m) and all island life, were devastated by vast pyroclastic flows from the eruption of the Lake Taupo caldera in 180 CE. Luckily, the first human inhabitants did not occupy the island until 1000 CE.

Around 200 black bears were killed in the eruption of Mount St Helens

The effects of a volcano can be disastrous for wildlife. Figures from Mount St Helens estimate that 11,000 hares, 6,000 deer, 5,200 elk, 1,400 coyotes, 300 bobcats, 200 black bears, and 15 mountain lions were killed by the blast.

The burning clouds of pyroclastic flows can travel at terrifying speeds of up to 500 kph (300 mph) and reach temperatures of 800°C (1,472°F), burning everything in their path.

A truck flees from the burning clouds of Pinatubo, Philippines, 1991

At Pinatubo, pyroclastic flows travelling at over 70 kph (40 mph) were recorded.

Where cracks form in the ocean floor as tectonic plates move apart, the water heated by the magma can reach temperatures of 662°C (1,224 °F).

One of Iceland's greatest attractions used to be the Great Geyser, near Reykjavik, which had a jet 60-80 m (200-270 ft) high. When the geyser stopped spouting in 1916, people managed to reactivate it a few times using soap powder, but it is now just an 18 m (60 ft) hole.

In 1883, when Krakatau, in Indonesia, erupted, the noise was so powerful it burst the eardrums of sailors over 40 km (25 miles) away. Around 36,000 people died, most killed by the tsunamis – some 30 m (100 ft) tall – that devastated Java and Sumatra. Villages, ships, and boats were swept inland, including a large steamer, which was found 2.6 km (1.5 miles) inland.

Fires are a major problem after an earthquake. Fractured gas pipes mean fires spread rapidly and burst water mains dry up the hoses. This, together with streets blocked with debris, make the firefighters' work near impossible.

The greatest volcanic eruption in modern times was Tambora, Indonesia, in 1815. It produced 80 km^3 (19.2 miles^3) of volcanic ash, compared with just 1 km^3 (0.24 miles^3) measured at Mount St Helens. In the last 10,000 years only four eruptions have been as violent as Tambora.

In the open ocean a tsunami can travel at incredible speeds of up to 600 kph (373 mph).

A steamer swept inland after Krakatau erupted

Animals often show strange behaviour before an earthquake. In 1975 in China, scientists successfully predicted an earthquake when they noticed snakes waking up from hibernation and rats swarming.

Q When is a volcano said to be extinct rather than dormant?

A Scientists put volcanoes into three categories. A volcano is classified as active if it has erupted within the last few hundred years. It is dormant if it has not erupted in the last few hundred years but has erupted during the last several thousand years. If a volcano has not erupted during the last several thousand years it is said to be extinct.

Q Are earthquakes high on the Richter scale the most destructive?

A Not necessarily – all sorts of factors influence the effects of a quake, the geology of the rock, in particular. Increasingly, earthquakes are measured on a scale called Moment magnitude. This combines Richter readings with observations of rock movement to give a more accurate scale of destruction.

Q How many active volcanoes are there in the world?

A There are more than 1,500 active volcanoes in the world that rise above sea level. On average, each month around 20–30 are actually erupting. Some of these are volcanoes that erupt continually, like the Hawaiian volcanoes of Mauna Loa and Kilauea.

Earthquake drill at a school in the USA

Q What should you do if there is an earthquake?

A At home, shelter in a doorway or under a strong table. In a public place, such as a classroom, find cover under a table or desk and protect your head with your arms. When the tremors stop, leave the building, and shelter as far as possible from walls, which may be unstable.

Q Have people ever tried to stop advancing lava flow?

A When the volcano on the Icelandic island of Heimaey erupted in 1973, the people tried to save the harbour on which the island depended from the lava. They did not stop it, but by spraying 6 million tonnes of sea water at the lava, they slowed it down and slightly altered its course. The lava flow stopped just 137 m (450 ft) from the harbour.

Mauna Loa, Hawaii

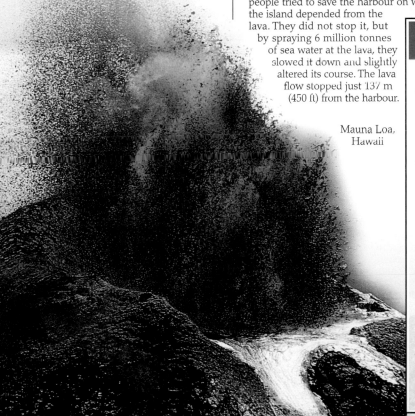

Q Could lava just come out of a crack in the earth?

A Yes, in 1943, in Paricutin in Mexico, a farmer found lava pouring from a crack that suddenly appeared in his field. Within a day there was a cone 10 m (33 ft) high. With eruptions over the following months, Paricutin grew layer by layer. After one year the lava was 450 m (1,476 ft) tall and had engulfed the nearby town.

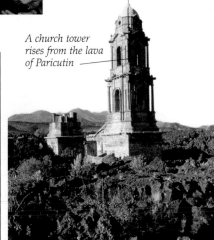

A church tower rises from the lava of Paricutin

A town buried by lava, Paricutin, Mexico

Record Breakers

BIGGEST VOLCANO
Mauna Kea in Hawaii is a massive volcano, 1,355 m (4,446 ft) taller than Mount Everest, but because it rises out of the sea bed, much of it is covered by sea water.

TALLEST GEYSER
The world's tallest geyser is the Steamboat Geyser in Yellowstone Park, Wyoming, USA. with spray up to 60-115 m (195-380 ft). But in 1904, Waimangu Geyser, New Zealand, reached a height of 460 m (1,500 ft).

BIGGEST EARTHQUAKE
In 1960 an earthquake with a magnitude of 9.5 on the Richter scale was recorded in Chile. It caused tsunamis which reached Japan.

MOST DEVASTATING EARTHQUAKE
In 1556 an earthquake of 8.3 on the Richter scale killed 800,000 people in Shansi, China.

HIGHEST TSUNAMI WAVE
The highest tsunami wave recorded struck Ishigaki in Japan in 1971. The monstrous wave was 85 m (279 ft) high.

Timeline

OUR PLANET HAS A VIOLENT HISTORY and its constant activity continues to remind us that we live at the mercy of the natural world. The timeline below includes just some of the major volcanic eruptions and earthquakes of the past four thousand years. We have most information about events in living memory or from records in recent history, but volcanologists can look much further back in time by studying the features of the Earth's surface. It is thought that one of the biggest eruptions ever happened two million years ago in Yellowstone, Wyoming and was 250 times more powerful than that of Pinatubo in 1991.

Gas, dust and rock explode
from Mount St Helens, 1980

C. 1620 BCE SANTORINI, GREECE
Violent eruptions blew the island of Santorini apart and buried it under 30 m (98 ft) of pumice.

79 CE VESUVIUS, ITALY
A burning cloud of volcanic ash engulfed the Roman towns of Pompeii and Herculaneum killing thousands.

1755 LISBON, PORTUGAL
A powerful earthquake measuring 8.5 on the Richter scale shook Portugal's capital, reducing it to rubble.

1783 SKAFTAR FIRES, ICELAND
A fissure (crack) 27 km (16 miles) long opened up in the Earth's surface, spewing out poisonous gases and red-hot lava.

Craters mark Skaftar fissure today

1815 TAMBORA, INDONESIA
The biggest eruption ever recorded. Around 90,000 Indonesians were killed. It is believed that the dust ejected reduced levels of sunlight around the world and affected the climate of the planet dramatically.

1883 KRAKATAU, INDONESIA
The enormous force of Krakatau's eruption left a crater 290 m (960 ft) deep in the ocean floor and created huge tsunamis that devastated the coastlines of Java and Sumatra.

1902 MOUNT PELÉE, MARTINIQUE
All but two of the entire population of St Pierre were wiped out by the burning cloud of gas and dust that raced down the sides of Mount Pelée at speeds of 161 kph (100 mph). Around 30,000 people died.

1906 SAN FRANCISCO, USA
Two huge earth tremors hit the city setting off fires that burned for many days. The earthquake is estimated to have measured 8.3 on the Richter scale.

1920 XINING, CHINA
The entire province of Gansu was devastated when shaken by an earthquake measuring 8.6 on the Richter scale. Over 180,000 people were killed.

1923 TOKYO, JAPAN
An earthquake of 8.3 on the Richter scale flattened 600,000 homes and knocked over stoves, which started a terrible firestorm.

A watch stopped by the eruption of Mount Pelée, 1902

1943 PARICUTIN, MEXICO
Lava began to flow from a crack that appeared in a farmer's field. By 1952 the cone stood 528 m (1,732 ft) tall.

1963 SURTSEY, ICELAND
Undersea volcanic explosions created a new island off the southwest coast of Iceland.

1963 SKOPJE, MACEDONIA
A violent earthquake destroyed more than 15,000 homes leaving three-quarters of the town of Skopje homeless. At least 1,000 people were killed.

The ruins of San Francisco, 1906

Cinders engulf Vestmannaeyjar, Iceland

1973 HEIMAEY, ICELAND
Eldfell volcano erupted after 5,000 years of dormancy. Molten lava engulfed one third of the town of Vestmannaeyjar on the Icelandic island of Heimaey.

1976 TANGSHAN, CHINA
The most disastrous earthquake in modern times. A massive tremor of 8.3 on the Richter scale almost completely destroyed the city of Tangshan and killed over 240,000 people.

1980 MOUNT ST HELENS, USA
The eruption of Mount St Helens sent gas, ash, and rock hurtling down the mountainside, devasting vast areas around the volcano.

1985 MEXICO CITY, MEXICO
Powerful earth tremors, measuring 8.1 on the Richter scale, shook Mexico City for three minutes. High-rise buildings in the city centre crashed to the ground. One million people were left homeless.

1985 NEVADO DEL RUIZ, COLOMBIA
The eruption of the Ruiz volcano caused a massive mudflow which engulfed the town of Armero 60 km (36 miles) away and buried 22,000 people in the mud.

1988 SPITAK, ARMENIA
Armenia and northeastern Turkey were shaken by a powerful earth tremor which almost completely destroyed the town of Spitak and killed most of the population.

1991 KILAUEA, HAWAII
Kilauea volcano, gently active since 1983, suddenly produced large quantities of lava which buried 13 km (8 miles) of road, 181 homes, and a visitors' centre.

1991 PINATUBO, PHILIPPINES
The most violent volcanic eruption of the twentieth century. Falling ash destroyed 42,000 homes and smothered land. Volcanic ash in the atmosphere lowered temperatures around the world.

1994 LOS ANGELES, USA
An earthquake under the city destroyed nine highways and 11,000 buildings in 30 seconds.

1995 KOBE, JAPAN
Kobe was badly damaged by the most powerful earthquake to hit a modern city, measuring 7.2 on the Richter scale. Buildings were also damaged in Kyoto 50 km (40 miles) away.

1996 GRIMSVOTN, ICELAND
A 4-km (2.5-mile) long fissure appeared in the side of the Grimsvotn volcano, which lies below the Vatnajökull glacier in Iceland. Lava melting the glacier ice caused terrible flooding, which damaged roads, pipelines, and power cables.

1997 MONTSERRAT, ANTILLES
A series of major eruptions left two-thirds of the island of Montserrat uninhabitable, forcing 8,000 people to leave.

1998 NEW GUINEA
A violent offshore earthquake caused a 10-m (33-ft) high tsunami, which swept 2 km (1.2 miles) inland. Around 4,500 people died.

The destruction of the expressway, Kobe, Japan

2002 DEMOCRATIC REPUBLIC OF CONGO
About half a million people were forced to leave their homes when rivers of lava flowed from Mount Nyiragongo. The lava took a blazing path through Goma, destroying two-fifths of the town.

2004 SUMATRA-ANDAMAN, INDIAN OCEAN
An undersea earthquake, with an epicentre just off the west coast of Sumatra, Indonesia, triggered a series of tsunamis, killing around 187,000 people.

2005 PAKISTAN
Also known as the Kashmir earthquake, this violent quake, measuring 7.6 on the Richter scale, killed around 73,000 people and left 33 million homeless.

Kilauea volcano, Hawaii

Find out more

VOLCANOES ARE EXTREMELY UNPREDICTABLE and even experienced volcanologists have been killed in eruptions. However, there are volcanic national parks all over the world where you can see volcanic features safely, at first hand. There are also more accessible ways to find out more about volcanoes, including sites on the Internet where you can find news of the latest eruptions and even watch volcanic activity live.

YELLOWSTONE PARK, USA
A line of people can be seen here walking through the lunar-like landscape of Norris geyser basin in Yellowstone National Park, Wyoming, USA. Yellowstone lies on a volcanic hot spot and has a dramatic landscape with volcanic features such as geysers and fumaroles. It also experiences earthquakes. The park's most famous feature is the geyser named "Old Faithful".

THE STORY OF AN ERUPTION
The remains of the ancient cities of Pompeii and Herculaneum, near Naples, in Italy (see pages 26–32), have not only taught scientists a lot about volcanoes but they also give visitors invaluable insight into both volcanoes and life in ancient Roman times. Both cities were destroyed when Vesuvius erupted in 79 CE, but the mountain is still an active volcano – it last erupted in 1944. Weather permitting, visitors can climb up and look into the crater of the volcano.

The bodies of ancient Romans suffocated by the poisonous gases were preserved in the volcanic ash

The ruins of Pompeii lying in the shadow of Vesuvius

Places to visit

THE EARTH GALLERIES, THE NATURAL HISTORY MUSEUM, LONDON
Displays on volcanoes and earthquakes and the chance to experience an earthquake for yourself.

ETNA, VESUVIUS, AND STROMBOLI, ITALY
The best-known of the Italian volcanoes are Etna in Sicily, the island of Stromboli, and Vesuvius near Naples. All can be climbed with guides, weather and volcanic activity permitting.

THE CANARY ISLANDS
Volcanic features dominate the Canary Islands. Tourists can visit the active volcano on La Palma and the volcanic landscape of Lanzerote.

ICELAND
Iceland is still being formed by volcanic activity and has over two dozen volcanoes, but is most famous for its geysers and hot springs.

Runny pahoehoe lava flowing over a cliff made up of layer upon layer of lava

VISITING VOLCANOES
There are national parks worldwide where visitors can see signs of volcanic activity, past and present. Some of the best known are in Hawaii, mainland USA, Iceland, New Zealand, Japan, Mexico, and the Canary Islands. In Hawaii, there is almost constant volcanic activity. Visitors can drive to the rim of the active volcano, Kilauea, walk through a lava tube, and see an eruption from a safe distance.

Lava flow from Kilauea volcano in Hawaii

WATCHING THE EARTH

Bᴇᴄᴀᴜѕᴇ ᴏf ᴛʜᴇ ᴅᴀɴɢᴇʀѕ, only trained volcanologists can monitor volcanoes closely, but on the Internet you can follow much of the work that such experts are doing all over the world. In the box below you will find the addresses of some websites with general background information on volcanology and links to lots of specific volcanoes. Some sites even have "volcanocams" so that you can watch volcanoes live, or almost live, on-line. For the most up-to-date information, the Smithsonian Institution in the USA produces an on-line weekly report on volcanic activity worldwide.

LIVING WITH A VOLCANO
These children are learning about Sakurajima volcano in Japan. It is one of the most active volcanoes in the world, erupting around 150 times a year. Like many other active volcanoes, Sakurajima is monitored by a volcano observatory which collects data for research and to help predict activity that might endanger people's lives. Most observatories have websites with the latest information and pictures.

WATCHING FROM SPACE
This picture was taken by a Space Shuttle and shows thick clouds of ash and dust from the eruption of Kliuchevskoi volcano in Russia, in 1994. Volcanic ash clouds can cause pollution and affect climate and aviation. They are watched and measured by satellites. Amazing views of volcanoes on Earth and in space can be found on several websites.

USEFUL WEBSITES

- An introduction to volcanoes by Michigan Technical University: **www.geo.mtu.edu/volcanoes/**
- Worldwide volcanic reference map: **www.geo.mtu.edu/volcanoes/world.html**
- Smithsonian Institution report on volcanic activity: **www.volcano.si.edu/**
- US Geological Survey homepage with links to volcanoes: **www.usgs.gov/**
- NASA directory of links to natural hazards sites including volcanoes, earthquakes, and tsunamis: **gcmd.gsfc.nasa.gov/Resources/pointers/hazards.html**
- For amazing volcanic images and tips on how to build a volcano model: **http://volcano.und.nodak.edu**

DANGEROUS WORK
This volcanologist is checking gas samples inside the crater of Mount Erebus, Antarctica. It is dangerous work and in recent decades several volcanologists have been killed by unexpected eruptions. But this is just a small part of a volcanologist's work. Much more time is spent analysing the data and advising people on the risks associated with volcanoes. There are lots of sites on the internet where you can learn more about a volcanologist's work and find out how to become one.

Glossary

AA A Hawaiian word used to describe thick, lumpy lava that forms angular lumps when cool.

AFTERSHOCKS Smaller earth tremors that happen after an earthquake. These may occur for several days or even weeks after the main tremor.

ASH AND DUST In volcanology, these terms refer to the smallest fragments of lava formed when a volcano explodes. Small pieces are called ash, and the powder-fine particles are known as dust.

BASALT The most common volcanic rock. Basalt is formed by runny lavas and is dark and fine-grained.

BLACK SMOKER A volcanic hot spring on the ocean floor that spits out black water containing metal sulphides and oxides.

BOMBS AND BLOCKS Large pieces of lava that are thrown out during a volcanic eruption. Bombs are slightly rounded in shape, while blocks are more angular.

CALDERA A giant crater or bowl-shaped depression at the top of a volcano, formed when the summit collapses into the volcano's magma chamber. Calderas can be many miles across.

CARBONISE To turn to carbon. Objects that contain carbon will turn to carbon (or charcoal), rather than burn, when there is not enough oxygen available for them to burn in the usual way.

Carbonised walnuts from Pompeii

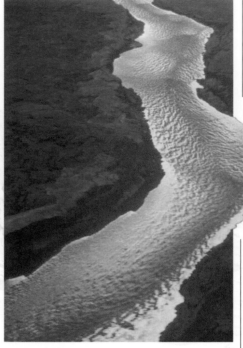

A red-hot flow of aa lava, Hawaii

CONTINENTAL DRIFT Continent movement caused by plate tectonics.

CORE The centre of the Earth, made up of dense metals, in particular iron. The inner core is solid while the outer core is liquid metal.

CRATER Hollow depression formed when the cone of a volcano collapses inwards. Also known as a caldera.

CRATER LAKE Lake formed when water fills the crater or caldera of a volcano.

DORMANT The term used to describe a volcano that has not been active for more than several hundred years but was active within the last several thousand years.

The crater of Mount Vesuvius, Italy

EPICENTRE The point on the Earth's surface, directly above the focus, or point of origin, of an earthquake.

EXTINCT The term used to describe a volcano that has not been active for over several thousand years.

FAULT A fracture in rock along which blocks of rock slide past each other.

FEEDER PIPE The long tube magma passes through from the magma chamber to the surface.

FISSURE A crack in the ground. A fissure eruption is one where runny lava flows from a crack in the ground.

FOCUS The point within the Earth's mantle from which an earthquake originates.

A geyser in Iceland

FUMAROLE A vent or opening in the Earth's surface that emits steam or gas.

GEOLOGY The study of the history and development of Earth's rocks and past life.

GEYSER A place where water that has been superheated by hot magma underground bursts up into the air.

HOT SPOT A place in the middle of a tectonic plate, rather than at the boundary, where columns of magma from the mantle rise up through the crust creating a volcano.

HYDROTHERMAL VENT A place where mineral-rich water heated by hot magma underground erupts onto the surface. Geysers, black smokers, and hot springs are all hydrothermal vents.

IGNEOUS ROCKS Rocks formed as hot magma and lava cools.

INTENSITY The term used to describe the severity of the shaking experienced during an earthquake. It is usually measured using the Modified Mercalli Intensity Scale.

LAHAR A mudflow made up of large quantities of volcanic fragments and water. Also known as a mudflow.

LAPILLI Small fragments of lava, formed as the magma bursts out of a volcano.

LAVA Hot, molten rock that is emitted from a volcano.

LAVA TUBE A tunnel of lava created when the surface of a lava flow cools and hardens to form a roof, while hot, molten lava continues to flow inside it.

MAGMA Hot, molten rock originating from within Earth.

MAGMA CHAMBER Area beneath a volcano where magma builds up before an eruption.

MAGNITUDE The term used to describe the severity or scale of an earthquake. This is calculated or measured in several different ways, the most common of which is the Richter scale.

Aa lava

MANTLE The layer inside the Earth between the crust and the core. The mantle is 2,900 km (1,800 miles) thick.

MERCALLI SCALE The scale for measuring the intensity of an earthquake by observing its effects.

MID-OCEAN RIDGE A mountain ridge on the ocean floor formed where two tectonic plates meet.

MUDFLOW A fast-moving stream of mud, water, and often volcanic ash and pumice. Also known as a lahar.

NUEE ARDENTE French for "glowing cloud". The term used to describe the strange clouds of a pyroclastic flow when they are a mix of cloud and hot ash.

PAHOEHOE The Hawaiian term for hot, runny lava that flows quickly and, usually, in quite shallow flows.

Pahoehoe lava

PILLOW LAVA Rounded lava formations shaped when lava erupts gently underwater.

PLATE TECTONICS The theory that the Earth's surface is broken up into large slabs or plates. The seven large plates and various smaller plates are constantly moving at the rate of a few centimetres a year. Most volcanoes and earthquakes are found at the boundaries of these plates.

Seismogram of the 1923 Tokyo earthquake

PLUG An obstruction of solidified magma in the neck of a volcano.

PUMICE Lightweight volcanic rock filled with holes formed by the bubbles of gas in the lava.

PYROCLASTIC FLOW A burning cloud of gas, dust, ash, rocks, and bombs that flows down the mountain after an explosive eruption. If the cloud is made up of more gas than ash it is known as a pyroclastic surge.

P WAVES The fastest and first or "primary" waves of an earthquake.

RICHTER SCALE Scale for measuring the total energy released by earthquakes and recorded seismographs. The scale ranges from 1 to 10, with 10 the most severe end of the scale. Each whole number increase corresponds to an increase of about 32 times the amount of energy released.

Pumice

RING OF FIRE The area encircling the Pacific Ocean where most volcanic and earthquake activity occurs.

SEISMIC WAVES The vibrations, or shock waves, that radiate out from the focus of an earthquake.

SEISMOMETER A machine for detecting earthquake shock waves is called a seismometer. A machine that records the information is called a seismograph.

SEISMOGRAM The record produced by a seismograph showing the pattern of shock waves from an earthquake.

SUBDUCTION ZONE Where two tectonic plates meet and one plate is pushed down into the mantle, partially melting rocks. The resulting magma erupts at the surface through volcanoes.

S WAVES The slower, "secondary" waves of an earthquake.

TSUNAMI Fast-moving waves caused by earthquakes or volcanic eruption displacing the ocean floor and water.

VENT The opening through which a volcanic eruption occurs.

VOLCANOLOGIST A scientist who studies volcanoes.

Volcanologists collecting gas samples on Colima volcano, in Mexico

Index

Acknowledgements

Dorling Kindersley would like to thank:
John Lepine & Jane Insley of the Science Museum, London; Robert Symes, Colin Keates & Tim Parmenter of the Natural History Museum, London; the staff at the Museo Archeologico di Napoli; Giuseppe Luongo, Luigi Iadicicco & Vincenzo D'Errico at the Vesuvius Observatory for help in photographing the instruments on pp. 49, 53 & 55; Paul Arthur; Paul Cole; Lina Ferrante at Pompeii; Dott. Angarano at Solfatara; Carlo Illario at Herculaneum; Roger Musson of the British Geological Survey; Joe Cann; Tina Chambers for extra photography; Gin von Noorden & Helena Spiteri for editorial assistance; Céline Carez for research & development; Wilfred Wood & Earl Neish for design assistance; Jane Parker for the index; Stewart J. Wild for proof-reading; David Ekholm–JAlbum, Sunita Gahir, Susan St. Louis, Carey Scott, Lisa Stock, & Bulent Yusuf for the clipart; Neville Graham, Sue Nicholson, & Susan St. Louis for the wallchart.

Illustrations: John Woodcock

Maps: Sallie Alane Reason

Models: David Donkin (pp. 8–9, 50–51)& Edward Laurence Associates (pp. 12-13)

Picture credits
a-above; b-below; c-centre; l-left; r-right; t-top

Ancient Art & Architecture Collection: 47t. Art Directors Photo Library: 47tc, 49tc. B.F.I.: 46cr, 57cr. Bridgeman Art Library: 6tl & c. Musee des Beaux-Arts, Lille: 44tl. British Museum: 27tr & c. Herge/Casterman: 20tl. Dr Joe Cann, University of Leeds: 25bc. Jean-Loup Charmet: 27bl, 31tl, 46bl, 51tl. Circus World Museum, Baraboo, Wisconsin: 32br. Corbis: Bettmann 67tl; Danny Lehman 65cr;Vittoriano Rastelli 70tc; Roger Ressmeyer 71br; Jim Sugar Photography 67b. Eric Crichton: 41tr, 41bl. Culver Pictures Inc: 60br. DK Images: Satellite Imagemap © 1996–2003 Planetary Visions 9c. Earthquake Research Institute, University of Tokyo: 63cr. Edimedia/Russian Museum, Leningrad: 28cl. E.T. Archive: 49c, 58tr, 62tl. Mary Evans Picture Library: 8tc, 16tl, 26tl, 27br, 28c, 29cr, 46tl, 64cr, 66br. Le Figaro Magazine/ Philippe Bourseiller: 19t, 19cl 19bl, 19br, 35tr. Fiorepress: 49br. Gallimard: 44tr. Getty Images: 59bl. G.S.F.: 13tl, 14bl; /Frank Fitch 20c. John Guest c.NASA: 44bl. Robert Harding Picture Library: 12tl, 14tr, 15cr 17tr, 17cr, 20tr, 21br, 63br, 24tl, 38br, 39br, 40tr, 42c, 43br, 48br, 49bl, 51tr, 60lc, 62bl, 62–63c, Explorer 66bl. Bruce C. Heezen & Marie Tharp, 1977/c.Marie Tharp: 11c. Historical Pictures Service, Inc.: 10cr. Michael

Holford: 22tr. Illustrated London News: 60bl. ImageState: 68bc. Katz Pictures: Alberto Garcia/ Saba 64b. Frank Lane Picture Agency: 23rct, 23c. Frank Lane Picture Agency /S.Jonasson: 41tc, 49cr. Archive Larousse-Giraudon: 32cl. London Fire Brigade/LFCDA: 58bl. Mansell Collection: 31tr. NASA: 24bc, 55cr, 68-69. Natural History Museum: 34tl. National Maritime Museum: 8tl. Orion Press: 7tr, 61bl. Oxford Scientific Films/ Colin Monteath: 69br; /NASA: 69cl; /Kim Westerkov: 11bl; 15tl. PA Photos: Andy Eames/AP 57cl. Planet Earth Pictures/Franz J.Camenzind: 7cr; /D.Weisel: 17br; /James D. Watt: 23rcb; /Robert Hessler: 25tr, 25lc. Popperfoto: 6b, 11tl, 54tl. R.C.S. Rizzoli: 48lc. Rex Features: 67tr. Gary Rosenquist: 14tl, 14br, 15tr, 15br. Scala: 7c, 49bl(inset); /Louvre: 63tr. Science Photo Library/Earth Sattelite Corp.: 7tl; /Peter Menzel: 7br, 20br, 46cl, 65bl; /David Parker: 13tr, 61tl, 61tr, 65tc; /Ray Fairbanks: 18c; / Inst Oceanographic Sciences: 24c; /Matthew Shipp: 24bl; /NASA: 35c, 43cr, 44cr, 44c, 44-45b; / U.S.G.S.: 45tr; /Peter Ryan: 55tr; /David Weintraub 66t. Frank Spooner Pictures: 8cl, 16cr, 17tl, 22bl, 23tr, 23br, 35tc, 42cl, 47cl, 49cl, 56tl, 56c, 56bl, 57bl, 58tl, 59tr, 59br, 61lcb; /Nigel Hicks 69tr. Syndication International: 31cr; /Inst. Geological Science: 32tc, 35br, 41tl, 47br; /Daily Mirror: 54tr, 57tr. Susanna van Rose: 39bl. Woods Hole Oceanographic Institute/Rod Catanach: 24br; / Dudley Foster: 25bl; /J.Frederick Grassle: 25tc; /Robert Hessler: 25tl. ZEFA: 9tl, 21t, 34bl, 45br, 57br.

Wallchart: Corbis: Burstein Collection / Barney Burstein fbr; Roger Ressmeyer cra; DK Images: Museo Archeologico Nazionale di Napoli cr; Natural History Museum, London clb (aa lava), cra (pyroclastic debris); Getty Images: Image Bank / G. Brad Lewis cla (Pahoehoe flow); National Geographic / Klaus Nigge ca; NASA: crb; Science Photo Library: Peter Menzel br (San Francisco)

All other images © Dorling Kindersley.
For further information see:
www.dkimages.com